# WORDS MATTER TODAY

## *57 Ways to Grow Confidence and Transform Experiences*

### Coach Mandy
Amanda Yetter

10-10-10
Publishing

# This Book is Dedicated

### To my husband

for choosing to be my life partner and my rock. Thank you for choosing to walk this incredible journey with me. Your unwavering belief in me and your constant support have allowed me to become the person I aspire to be each and every day. By your side, I have discovered how to receive and give love, achieve success, and find fulfillment. Together, we have built a strong foundation for our family. You are my best friend, my guiding light, and I am blessed to be in your arms. I am forever grateful for your presence in my life and for showing me the true meaning of love and companionship.

### To my children

for opening my heart in new ways, bringing true joy and laughter into my life, teaching me lessons on how to be there and let go at the same time, showing me what truly matters, and inspiring me to continually grow to be a better person than I was yesterday. To Marissa, for showing me the importance of investing time into discovering what I would love and lights me up to explore my dreams with my whole heart and real actions. To Jenna, for reminding me to be happy, give hugs, laugh loudly, and shine brightly every day. To Aarik, for investing time to listen and talk with me about my dreams, reminding me to pat myself on the back and celebrate progress in the actions I take in the direction of my dreams.

### To my precious grandchildren

those who grace our lives today and those to come, for shaping our future. May you carry the light of love, wisdom, and compassion to the next generations, inspiring a world of limitless possibilities.

### To my sisters and brothers

for always being there for each other, believing that we could do anything, and sharing in the journey of life itself together, with Becky reminding me I am smarter then I think, Carrie teaching me how to laugh and play full out, Kenny showing me love runs deep and to let everyone know I love them every chance I have, and Tommy for helping me see it is good to go all in on all I do.

### To my other brother, Jason

for teaching me love is way thicker than blood, helping me to see being there for someone is the most important thing you may ever do, and words do matter.

### To my extended family

for welcoming me with open arms as part of your families, for your love and for the support you give, reminding me that I am never alone. In times of joy, you celebrate alongside me, filling our hearts with laughter and precious memories. I am honored to call each and every one of you a cherished brother, sister, parent, uncle, aunt, cousin, and member of my family.

### To my grandparents

for loving me unconditionally with the best hugs in the world.

### To Granny Bev

for showing me life is full of surprises, and stories are the content of who we become.

### To my aunts

for always holding me close to your hearts and in your pocket with your love.

**To my uncles**

for your strength, support, love, and guidance, no matter the conditions.

**To my cousins**

for being the best friends in the world
and for the cherished moments we've shared.

**To my nieces and nephews**

for bringing even more joy and laughter into my life, and for reminding me
of the beauty of dreams and unlimited possibilities.

**To my friends**

for your unwavering support, acceptance, and for being there for me
in all that I am and all that I do. Thank you for allowing me
to do the same for you.

**To my teachers, coaches, and bosses**

for guiding me and changing my life with your wisdom,
mentorship, and belief in my potential.

**To my mentor, Pat Slowey**

for seeing my potential, trusting in my abilities, and guiding me to go for
what I want and do the right thing. Your belief in me and your unwavering
support have been invaluable on my journey. Above all, I am grateful for
your genuine care and concern for me and my family, showing me what a
leader is and how to care about who we work with, remembering to give
everyone a turn. Your mentorship has transformed my life.

**To my teammates**
for standing by my side every day, supporting
and encouraging me in all that we do together.

**To my clients**
for allowing me to be a part of your journey and for inspiring me
to write this book. Your trust and dedication have fueled my passion
to make a positive impact.

# Contents

# Foreword

Welcome to a transformative journey guided by an exceptional author and transformational coach Amanda Yetter, known as Coach Mandy. Get ready to embark on a profound exploration of the power of words, as you dive into the pages of *Words Matter Today: 57 Ways to Grow Confidence and Transform Experiences.*

In this extraordinary book, Coach Mandy invites you to discover the immense impact that your words have on your life, relationships, and overall well-being. With a deep understanding of the human spirit and the power of mindset, she weaves together insightful narratives and practical strategies that will empower you to embrace your authenticity, cultivate confidence, and unlock your true potential.

As you immerse yourself in the wisdom shared within these pages, you'll embark on a transformative journey of self-discovery and personal growth. Through the 57 empowering ways outlined in this book, Coach Mandy provides you with invaluable tools, exercises, and reflections to harness the power of your words and create a life filled with purpose, joy, and extraordinary achievements.

Drawing upon her own diverse experiences and triumphs over adversity, Coach Mandy's heartfelt guidance will resonate deeply within your heart. Her words will inspire, uplift, and ignite the spark of transformation, guiding you towards a path of self-empowerment and fulfillment.

With every chapter, you'll gain practical insights and actionable steps that will help you cultivate self-awareness, shift your perspective, and develop a positive mindset. Through engaging stories, thought-provoking exercises, and inspiring anecdotes, Coach Mandy illuminates the transformative potential that lies within you.

*Words Matter Today* is more than a book—it's a companion that will walk alongside you on your journey of personal growth. Whether you're seeking to enhance your relationships, boost your self-confidence, or create a more joyful and meaningful life, the wisdom within these pages will serve as your guide, offering practical tools and empowering insights every step of the way.

Now is the time to open your heart and mind, to uncover the incredible power of your words, and embark on a life-changing journey that will forever transform the way you think, speak, and experience the world around you.

**Raymond Aaron**
***New York Times* Bestselling Author**

# The Intention

Welcome to *Words Matter Today: 57 Ways to Grow Confidence and Transform Experiences*!

Discover the transformative power of words and their profound impact on your confidence, relationships, health, money, and career.

Have you ever felt trapped by self-doubt, plagued by negative self-talk, or held back from embracing new opportunities? The challenges of low confidence may be overwhelming, affecting your ability to fully enjoy and engage in experiences. Know this: There is a way for you to grow and move beyond those thoughts that hold you back.

My intention is to awaken your awareness of the vital significance of words in today's world and empower you with insights into the word patterns that directly shape your thoughts, feelings, actions, and results. Through this understanding, you cultivate unwavering confidence and manifest extraordinary outcomes.

Imagine breaking free from the grip of self-doubt and negative self-talk. Picture yourself embracing experiences with a renewed sense of self-assurance, free from the fear of judgment or criticism. What if you could confidently step outside your comfort zone and seize new opportunities for personal growth? It's time to redefine your boundaries and prioritize your well-being.

Within these pages, dive deep into the challenges arising from a lack of confidence and reveal practical solutions to overcome them. Drawing from extensive research, personal experiences, and the wisdom of those who have transformed their lives, inside there are 57 powerful strategies to help you rewrite your narrative and begin to unlock your full potential.

Learn how to silence your inner critic, challenge self-limiting beliefs, and cultivate self-compassion. Break free from the comparison trap and envy that overshadow your experiences. Learn to set healthy boundaries, prioritize self-care, and build resilience in the face of setbacks. By embracing these transformative strategies, you'll gain the confidence to fully engage, enjoy, and appreciate every aspect of your life.

At its core, the psychology is simple yet profound. Your thoughts shape your feelings, which drive your actions or inactions, and ultimately determine your results. To understand your thoughts, look no further than your results.

Unleash the power within you and shatter the chains of negative thinking. Are you ready to embrace a life filled with success, joy, and boundless possibilities? It all begins with a simple choice—to break free from the grip of negative thoughts that hold you back.

Imagine a world where doubt and self-limiting beliefs no longer have a hold on you. Picture yourself confidently pursuing your dreams, achieving your goals, and living a life of abundance. It's time to release the shackles of negativity and step into your full potential.

Negative thinking is contagious, infecting every aspect of your life and robbing you of the greatness you were meant to achieve. Here's the secret: You have the power to change it. By recognizing the impact of negative thoughts and actively choosing a different path, you transform your reality and become the best version of yourself.

Believe in the extraordinary possibilities that await you. Break free from the chains of negativity and embark on a journey of self-discovery, personal growth, and unlimited success. It's time to rewrite the narrative and create a future that exceeds your wildest dreams.

Are you ready to make the choice that will transform your life? Step into the realm of positivity, abundance, and self-belief. The journey starts now, and the destination is a life of unparalleled fulfillment. Embrace the power within you, and together, let's conquer the obstacles, unlock your potential, and achieve the success you deserve.

In a world where everything is energy, positive words radiate vibrancy and power, while negative words drain it. Discover if you are inadvertently using negative words and begin your personal journey to eliminate them altogether.

As a coach, business leader, and lifelong learner committed to personal development, I have witnessed the science and art of language transforming thoughts, feelings, actions, and results. It brings me great joy to share this knowledge with you to help create a new universal language and pattern of words that revolutionize your life experiences and shape a better future for everyone.

Uncover the 57 ways to immediately grow confidence and transform your life experiences. Let's radiate the power of words and embark on this life-changing voyage of personal growth.

# CHAPTER ONE

# You Have the Power

*"If you think you can, or you think you can't,*
*either way you are right."*
— Henry Ford

## 1. Choose Your Own Words

ife is a journey, and mine began on a farm. It was there that my mother taught me a valuable lesson about the power we each possess—the power to choose your thoughts and words. She showed me how your thoughts, words, feelings, and even the tone of your voice carry energy that shifts your confidence and transforms your experiences.

One memorable experience on the farm involved a group of baby ducklings encountering grass for the first time on a cold spring morning. The ducklings were scared, trembling like leaves, and frozen in the grass, unable to eat. My mother asked me to assist. Naturally, I felt a sense of joy in helping these little creatures.

She instructed me to sit quietly in the grass with the ducklings, to think calming thoughts, and to speak kind words to them. As I followed her guidance, I noticed their heads tilting as if they were listening, and magically, their breathing slowed. Their eyes softened, and they cautiously approached me. They allowed me to touch them, responding to my gentle words and touch. Then I guided them towards a bowl of food, where they eagerly began to eat. Afterward, they played together in the grass, eventually settling down for a restful nap.

My mother explained, "Mandy, you have the power to choose your thoughts and words. Your words are a reflection of your thoughts, and together, they shape how you feel. All of this carries energy that impacts you and everyone around you."

She went on to say that the positive energy I created was transferred to the baby ducklings. This positive energy instilled confidence in them, transforming their initial fear of the new environment into joy. It was a lesson that left me feeling special and empowered, knowing that each of us possesses this remarkable ability to experience immense joy and help others.

I discovered that if my words were loving, the response I received was love. I witnessed the baby ducklings' eyes soften, their breathing change, and a sense of calmness wash over them as they approached me. I had created a greater sense of peace for myself and a connection of love and joy between us in that moment. The same held true for all the farm animals—horses, cows, dogs, cats, ducks—they all responded to the power of positive words.

The key lesson here is that you have the power to choose your approach, and it all begins with the combination of your thoughts and words as an expression of yourself. Your words, as a reflection of your thoughts, hold great significance.

It is worth noting that the relationship between words and thoughts is certainly more than a one-way street and is rather a complex interplay. Your thoughts influence the words you choose, and in turn, the words you use influence your thoughts. Additionally, non-verbal forms of communication, such as gestures and facial expressions, play a role in expressing and shaping thoughts.

As a young child, I realized that I had the power to grow in confidence, transform experiences, and help others do the same through the words I chose. The key was in the decision of which words to choose. As I continued to grow in experiences, I learned more about how words and thoughts interact and reflect each other in various ways. Here are two perspectives to consider:

**Words as a Reflection of Thoughts:** According to this viewpoint, thoughts are seen as the primary source, and words are used to express and communicate those thoughts. In this sense, words are considered a reflection of our inner mental processes. Before you articulate your thoughts, you typically form them in your mind. Words serve as tools to externalize and convey those thoughts to others. From this perspective, words are secondary to thoughts and are used to convey our pre-existing ideas.

**Thoughts as a Reflection of Words:** Conversely, thoughts may be shaped and influenced by the words you use. Language plays a crucial role in shaping your cognitive processes and conceptual frameworks. The words you learn, the language structures you use, and the cultural context in which you operate may influence how you think. This perspective suggests that the words you use express your thoughts and shape and structure them. In this view, language acts as a cognitive tool that shapes your thinking processes.

As you read on, enjoy exploring this dynamic relationship. Consider how your thoughts shape your choice of words and vice versa. Additionally, explore how the words and word patterns you choose influence your thought processes and worldview.

## 2. Notice the Power of Words

**Have you ever considered the power of words?**

Let's delve deeper into this concept.

Take a moment to consider the statement, "Sticks and stones may break my bones, but words will never hurt me."

Perhaps you were taught this phrase as a way to defend yourself when someone said something hurtful. The intention behind this learned response is to stand up against those who intend to upset you, in the hopes that they cease. I, too, learned it this way.

The truth is that words do possess the power to hurt. The good news is that words do also have the power to uplift and inspire.

**What grants words such power?**

Energy. If you assume that everything is energy, then words become a source of it. In fact, words may be the most powerful form of energy. Think about it; words are utilized throughout every minute of your day. You use them to speak, write, text, read, and think. The same goes for everyone else in the world. Therefore, there is a stream of constant usage of words to direct and influence each other.

Consider this: What if words have the ability to raise or lower the frequency of our emotions?

Take a moment to reflect on the words you say or hear. Do you notice any difference in how you feel?

**Remember the story of the baby ducklings?**

If, instead, I had approached the baby ducklings with loud, angry words filled with frustration or rushed impatience, they would have responded by running away or squirming if I tried to pick them up.

Throughout the years of working with farm animals, I consistently witnessed the same results. It all began with the approach of the person, and the animals responded accordingly. Curiously, over the years, I observed family members and friends interacting with one another, witnessing the same pattern. This held true in my business experiences as well.

Here's an example for you to consider:

If someone said, "You are not good enough," how would you feel? Would you experience negative, threatened, contractive feelings, or even a sense of anger or sadness?

On the other hand, if someone said, "You are loved," how would you feel? Would you sense a positive, safe, expansive feeling or a sense of happiness?

*CAUTION: You may be someone who is motivated by the words, "You are not good enough to do this." Let's set aside those thoughts for the moment, as this type of energy is to be discussed in the next section.

The truth is, there is a noticeable difference in the emotions evoked by these words. You may find that these words are ones you say to yourself as self-talk or words you hear from others. Either way, they create a distinct feeling within you. Pay attention to these feelings and use them as a guide to help you choose words that bring about the highest level of positive energy.

As you embark on considering the words you choose, a good initial step is to notice how those words impact your emotions. You may find it helpful to begin keeping notes on words that generate positive and negative feelings for you. Grab a sheet of paper and create two columns with titles like negative & positive, sadness & happiness, contractive & expansive, or disempowering & empowering, etc.—whatever resonates with you. Take action to make a list of words that elicit feelings and categorize them to increase your awareness of the words you prefer based on how they make you feel.

HELPFUL HINT: Pay attention to statements containing the word "NOT," and write an opposite statement next to it. Through my experience working with clients, I have found this to be the easiest way to identify how energy is associated to words and how you feel. It turns out that statements with the word "NOT" are negative by nature and more common than you might think!

| Negative/Disempowering | Positive/Empowering |
|---|---|
| I am NOT good enough. | I am loved. |
| I am NOT ready. | I am ready. |
| I do NOT like chicken. | I do like pizza. |

# BONUS:

GROW CONFIDENCE, TRANSFORM EXPERIENCES, AND SHAPE YOUR FUTURE WITH THE POWER OF WORDS

**CLAIM YOUR FREE BONUS,** WORDS MATTER TODAY: YOUR GUIDE TO POWERFUL WORD CHOICES, by visiting www.WordsMatterToday.com to DOWNLOAD YOUR FULL-SIZE, FULL-COLOR, PRINT-READY VERSION.

The most powerful statement you may ever make is whatever comes after the words "I am." These two simple words hold immense potential to shape your reality and define your identity. Whether you say, "I am capable," "I am worthy," or "I am unstoppable," you are declaring your truth and affirming the limitless possibilities within you. Your self-perception, beliefs, and actions are all influenced by the words that follow "I am." So, choose your words wisely and intentionally, for they have the power to transform your life and manifest the extraordinary person you are meant to be. Embrace the power of "I am" and unleash the boundless potential that resides within you.

On the flip side, be aware of the tremendous impact that negative "I am" statements have on your life. When you say, "I am not good enough," "I am a failure," or "I am unworthy," you limit your potential and reinforce self-doubt. These self-deprecating words become the building blocks of a negative self-image and hinder your growth and happiness. Recognize that these statements are likely a product of conditioned thinking and past experiences and not a reflection of your true essence. Challenge and reframe these negative beliefs with empowering alternatives. Replace "I am not good enough," with "I am constantly growing and improving," and replace "I am a failure," with "I am resilient and capable of overcoming any challenge." By consciously choosing positive "I am" statements, you reshape your self-perception and open the door to a life filled with self-love, confidence, and unlimited possibilities.

Remember, the power of "I am" lies in your hands, so use it wisely to shape a future that aligns with your true potential.

One of the most profound moments of this type of shift that still resonates with me occurred during a heartfelt conversation with a teammate on a particularly challenging day. Tears were streaming down her face as she shared her struggles, saying, "I am having a breakdown." In that instant, without hesitation, I felt an overwhelming surge of empowerment and reassurance, and I replied with heartfelt certainty, "No, you are having a BREAKTHROUGH!" The room filled with laughter, and beneath the lightheartedness, there was a powerful truth that permeated the air. That transformational phrase, "I'm not having a breakdown; I am having a BREAKTHROUGH," became a defining moment in our journey together. It showcased the tremendous power of the words "I am," and how a simple shift in perspective can turn a challenging moment into an opportunity for growth and empowerment. This personal experience has become a core part of my coaching journey and a beacon of inspiration for all who seek to embrace their inner strength and transform adversity into triumph.

By raising your awareness and taking note of the words you use and how they make you feel, you begin to take steps in amplifying your power. This helps you decide which words to choose in order to boost your confidence and transform your daily experiences.

Now that you have begun to notice the power of words, you may start crossing off words from the list that create low energy and/or negative feelings. You may realize that you use or hear them frequently. This is because your awareness has increased, and you now notice what was previously overlooked. It's similar to when you decide to buy a new car, such as a white Honda Civic. Suddenly, you start seeing white Honda Civics everywhere! You begin to see how often certain words you use impact your energy.

The beauty of creating a list is that you visually observe your go-to words and how frequently you use them, both when speaking to others and in your own self-talk throughout the day. With heightened awareness of the words you have been using up until now, you possess the power to choose more of your favorite positive and empowering words, while reducing the presence of negative words you have crossed off the list.

The next step is to understand how the words you choose drive your experiences and shape your results.

## 3. Thoughts -> Feelings -> Actions -> Results

Within the realm of psychology, there exists a proven formula that helps us understand our results.

If...

**Thoughts -> Feelings -> Actions -> Results**

- Your results are an exact reflection of your thoughts.
- Your thoughts give rise to your feelings.
- Your feelings determine your actions or inactions.
- Your actions or inactions drive your results.

Therefore, your results are a direct manifestation of your thoughts.

- If you wish to comprehend your results, then direct your attention to your thoughts.

- If you find yourself lacking in financial abundance, observe your thoughts, and you may discover a focus on scarcity and lack of money.
- If you have achieved something remarkable, examine your thoughts, and you may find a firm belief in the possibility of success.

Consider the story of the Little Engine That Could, and the words used to grow thoughts to believe:

"I think I can. I think I can.
I know I can. I know I can.
I am. I am.
I did. I did.
I knew I could. I knew I could."

Do you see how the words fit into this formula of results?

Words are a reflection of your thoughts, and words may be used as a power tool to help shape your thoughts. In either case, they possess the power to raise or lower the frequency of your emotions. Take into account the following: If you repeatedly tell yourself, "I am NOT good enough; I am NOT ready," your thoughts become negative, and your words diminish the energy levels, eroding your confidence. Over time, this diminishes your ability to take action or leads to inaction, hindering your progress towards your goals.

Conversely, if you affirm to yourself, "I am loved, and I am ready," your thoughts become positive, and your words amplify high energy levels, bolstering your confidence and inspiring positive actions aligned with your goals. This amplifies your ability to achieve what you set out to accomplish.

The same principle applies when others use these words with you, or vice versa.

*CAVEAT: You may be someone who feels motivated by the words "You are not good enough to do this." While it may seem like a source of positive energy because it pushes you towards positive action, be wary of this type of motivation. It is known to steal JOY!

How do these types of words steal JOY? Words used to push you to do something are designed to be forceful and generally create a loss of freedom and limit choices—a "have to," which is an either/or contractive feeling—whereas words used to inspire you to do something are designed to open your thoughts up to ideas that pull you towards a vision and create freedom of choice, a YES/expansive feeling. Keeping with the example: "You are loved" lets you know that no matter what you do, you are loved. It is in the freedom of choice where you find the greatest JOY, because you are empowered to be yourself and do things because they are what you would love to do!

Notice the power you possess to choose words that generate:

**Positive Thoughts -> Positive Feelings -> Positive Actions -> Positive Results**

The transformative message within this section is for you to recognize how the results formula and the words you choose intertwine, empowering you to enhance both your CONFIDENCE and JOY throughout your experiences, at every stage of your thoughts, feelings, actions, and results.

Now that you have a solid understanding of how the results formula and your choice of words work in harmony, the next step is to identify patterns so that you may strengthen the positive patterns you desire.

## 4. Words Reflect Thought Patterns

Have you ever noticed how certain words or types of words seem to repeat themselves? Perhaps you've observed this within your own self-talk, or maybe you've noticed others consistently using the same words. Have you ever seen a pattern in the words you use or how you say them, depending on the people you're with?

Throughout my years of working with clients, I discovered a common pattern among them—they often express what they don't want before articulating what they do want. This pattern became apparent to me as I sought to understand their desires in order to provide guidance. The truth is, when you spend most of your time talking about what you don't want, there's little opportunity to focus on what you truly desire.

As I recognized this pattern in my clients and continued to develop my own life coaching programs, I became aware of this same pattern within myself. I noticed that I would often talk extensively about what I didn't want, and rarely mentioned what I did want.

As someone who has experienced my fair share of failed relationships, I understand firsthand how this pattern of focusing on what you don't want permeates your personal life. It took me a while to realize that by constantly dwelling on past disappointments and articulating what I didn't desire in a partner, I was inadvertently sabotaging my chances of experiencing the love and connection I truly craved. It was a profound moment of self-reflection when I recognized that my words held immense power in shaping my thoughts, and ultimately, my reality.

Why did I do this? Personally, I believe it was my way of safeguarding myself against disappointment. I thought that if I made it abundantly clear what I didn't want, others would understand my deepest fears and act differently. Perhaps it was a means of protecting myself from worst-case scenarios. Some may argue that this pattern of thinking stemmed from a broken heart, divorce, and the challenges of being a single parent—an attempt to control outcomes and shield myself from pain and letdown. Well, that's a story for another time...

The crucial point is that the pattern of my words was undeniably connected to my true thoughts. Despite yearning for positive change in my life, I used words to describe negative experiences that reflected my deepest fears, leaving little room to focus on the joy I longed for.

Today, if you or someone you know habitually starts conversations by highlighting what is NOT wanted, there is likely an underlying fear within their thoughts that gives rise to these words. This thought pattern becomes more apparent when words containing contractions, such as "don't" or "can't," are frequently used.

If you truly pay attention to your own speech patterns, you may discover recurring themes. Additionally, observing others' words may help you uncover patterns more easily. Listen attentively to what those around you say and how they say it. Do you notice any consistent patterns in their words? What do you discern as thought patterns behind their words? You may want to observe the written words you encounter, such as emails and texts. Do you identify any patterns in the messages you receive or send?

As you progress through the upcoming chapters, there are opportunities to delve deeper into specific words and the thought patterns that are passed down from generation to generation. For now, let's move on to the next section, where I explore the connection between results, thoughts, and, most importantly, the power of words and their connections to your thoughts. How may you effortlessly shift your thoughts through the words you choose today to achieve the results you truly desire?

## 5. Words Accelerate Results

Remember the powerful results formula discussed in the previous section:

- Your thoughts create how you feel.
- How you feel enables you to take or not take actions.
- Your actions or inactions drive your results.
- Therefore, your results ultimately equal your thoughts.

Now, imagine the liberation that comes with breaking free from self-imposed limitations and stepping outside of your comfort zone. By building confidence and aligning your thoughts with your desired results, you unlock a world of experiences and personal growth. The key lies in the words you choose today. As a reflection of your thoughts, you have the power to raise or lower the frequency of your feelings.

Think about it: Words originate from your imagination, a manifestation of your thoughts. When you have a goal or a desired result, you imagine it first. Then you translate that idea into words. Your choice of words affects how you feel about that result. The clearer and more precise your words, the stronger your vision becomes, igniting even more powerful thoughts and emotions aligned with your goals. These heightened feelings fuel the energy you need to take actions in pursuit of your desired results.

Words matter, because they hold immense power. They are the bridge between your thoughts and your reality. The words you choose today shape your thoughts, which in turn shape your results. Moreover, consciously selecting empowering words expands your thoughts, bringing them into closer alignment with your desired outcomes. This, in turn, amplifies your feelings and ignites the drive to take decisive actions. Your feelings and actions are the internal mechanisms propelling the wheel of achievement, determining the speed at which you attain your desired results.

By embracing the understanding that your words accelerate results, you hold the key to unlock the doors of liberation, confidence, and personal success. It is within your power to choose words that empower, inspire, and align with your desired outcomes. As you delve deeper into the following chapters, you may explore specific strategies to transform your words and revolutionize your results. Get ready to unleash the extraordinary possibilities that await when you harness the true power of your words.

## 6. As You Transform, Others Transform

As you continue reading and delve deeper into the transformative power of words today, you may find yourself naturally gravitating towards different choices in your own vocabulary. The knowledge you gain is meant to be shared with others. In fact, I encourage you to do so!

In the chapters ahead, you have a remarkable opportunity to expand your awareness of the power of words and discover new ways to consciously choose the language you use. It is my sincere pleasure to guide you through the impact of specific words, patterns, and phrases. My hope is that you wholeheartedly embrace what you learn, experience remarkable growth in your confidence and results, and then pay it forward by sharing these insights with others, empowering them to achieve the results they desire.

As Dale Carnegie once wisely said, "The only way on Earth to influence other people is to talk about what they want and show them how to get it."

By understanding and harnessing the power of your words, you embark on a personal transformation and unlock the potential to inspire and uplift those around you.

I acknowledge that the journey may be challenging at times. Patterns of thought and speech have been ingrained over generations and shape daily interactions. Like any entrenched behavior or habit, breaking free requires commitment and the ability to interrupt these patterns, replacing them with new, intentional choices in our words—whether spoken, written, or shared with others.

May the words you choose today become a beacon of light, both within yourself and for those around you. As you grow in confidence and authenticity, my wish for you is that you foster deeper connections and embrace life's experiences with a newfound sense of joy. Together, let us shine our lights brightly, living lives we love, and in doing so, let us create a transformative ripple effect that illuminates the world for generations to come.

# CHAPTER TWO

# Where Words Show Up

*"You are what you are, and you are where you are because of what has gone into your mind. You change what you are, and you change where you are by changing what goes into your mind."*
**– Zig Ziglar**

# CHAPTER TWO

## Where Words Show Up

## 7. Beware of Labels

Wat are labels and how do they affect us?

Labels are words or phrases used to organize thoughts or beliefs about a person. When used to describe individuals, labels may be inaccurate or restrictive, leading to negative consequences. Throughout your daily life, you may encounter labels given by you or by others. Labels shape perceptions and influence the way you interact with the world.

**Labeling and its impact on self-perception:**

Have you ever noticed how frequently labels are used? How often do you catch yourself using labels or hearing others use them? Labels like "lazy," "smart," "outgoing," or "shy" are examples of how people are categorized based on our perceptions and beliefs. However, these labels intentionally or unintentionally have a profound effect on individuals, especially those struggling with low confidence.

Consider the example of one of my clients, who I'll call Joe, who has been labeled by his parents as "lazy." Once labeled, Joe starts to internalize this belief, affecting how he feels about himself and his abilities. The label then influences his actions or lack thereof and ultimately the way others interact with him. As a result, Joe exhibits laziness, perpetuating the label and hindering his personal growth.

Similarly, imagine, as a young child, I was labeled as "shy." Over time, this label became deeply ingrained, impacting my behavior and preventing me from pursuing opportunities that require being outgoing. I conformed to societal expectations and restricted my true self, limiting my potential for personal growth. However, during my senior year, a pivotal moment occurred when my band director, Mr. Falvo, encouraged me to step out as a leader as captain of the silks team. The combination of the title of captain, Mr. Falvo's encouragement to be creative, and my mother's words of wisdom to fulfill the role's leadership requirements, helped me grow beyond the belief that I was ever truly shy. Truth be told, deep down, I always wanted to be a famous singer on the world's stage. My sisters and I would often pretend to be the Barbara Mandrell sisters, and we would imagine that we were performing for large crowds and on TV. So, maybe the label of being "shy," in some way, still holds me back from my dreams.

**Comparison and its impact on enjoyment:**

Labels affect individuals' self-perception and contribute to comparison and envy. People with low confidence often compare themselves to others, focusing on what they lack or what others possess. This constant comparison overshadows their ability to appreciate and enjoy their own experiences, leading to a diminished sense of fulfillment.

For instance, one of my clients, who I'll call Sally, was labeled as "smart." She felt immense pressure to constantly achieve high standards, leaving her feeling inadequate or never good enough. Similarly, her brother, as the oldest child, labeled himself as "outgoing," who she described as seeming to feel the need to fulfill others' expectations and often struggling to develop his own authentic identity.

**Becoming aware of labels and their effects:**

The power of a label, like any other word, lies in the ability to shape our thoughts and actions. It is crucial to be aware of the labels you place on yourself and others, particularly when it comes to children. Labels may be both accurate and inaccurate, so discerning which ones contribute to expansion and growth is essential.

To begin recognizing the labels placed on you by others, you may start by making a list of what people say about you. Additionally, engaging in an exercise like "About me & you" (as discussed in the next section) with trusted individuals, fosters deeper connections and provides insight into how others perceive you.

**Self-labeling and its impact on personal growth:**

Pay attention to the labels you place on yourself. The words you choose to describe your strengths, weaknesses, and identities shape your self-perception. Often, these self-labels may stem from fears and desires to protect yourself, and they may restrict your growth and keep you from fully embracing who you truly are.

Take a moment to reflect on your "I am" statements. Consider whether these statements raise or lower your energy levels. If uncertain, try listing opposite statements to test your energy response. For example, if you describe yourself as "shy," consider how it feels to label yourself as "outgoing" instead. It is important to note that neither of the labels are good or bad; it is how you feel about the label as you try it on.

**Rewriting labels and embracing personal empowerment:**

You have the power to change the labels you use, and the labels others place on you. By choosing your words wisely, you redefine how you perceive yourself and how others perceive you. Recognize the labels that empower you and those that cause contraction and discontent. Focus on embracing the labels that expand your true self and contribute to building confidence within you, because they describe who you want to be.

Throughout the next 24 hours, engage in an experiment of noticing where labels show up in your life. Observe how labels affect your emotions and drive your actions or lack thereof. By becoming aware of the impact labels have, you proactively create positive changes for yourself and others.

Are labels necessary? While labels are an inherent part of language and thought organization, you may use them consciously and purposefully. With awareness, labels may be a source of empowerment and help create more confidence and courage in an individual to embrace their true self.

**Exercise #1: Embracing your true self despite fears:**

To gain a deeper understanding of who you truly are, you are invited to complete the following exercise:

- Make a list of as many successes in your life as you recall. Remember the feeling associated with each success.
- Whenever thoughts or feelings of being undeserving arise, remind yourself of the feeling tone of those successful moments.
- Recognize the fears that may underlie your self-labels. Do your labels protect you from these fears, or do they keep you small?

- Challenge your self-labels by envisioning how they could be different. How would you like to change them?

Remember, you have the power to rewrite your own history and embrace your authentic self.

**Exercise #2: About me & you – Strengthening connections and celebrating strengths:**

This exercise serves as a powerful tool for fostering connections and self-reflection. It is designed to help individuals appreciate their positive attributes and gain insights into how others perceive them.

This exercise is designed to help you deepen your connection with others and celebrate your individual strengths, allowing you to connect with your truth and purpose.

- You do this exercise with 2 or more people.
- Each person takes a sheet of paper and writes their own name on it.
- On the front side of the paper, take a few minutes of silence to individually list all the positive words that describe yourself (estimated time: 1–2 minutes). It's recommended to play inspirational music during this time. Once done, flip the paper over.
- Choose one person to start as Person #1. Person #1 prepares to write on the backside of their own paper. The other participants then take turns saying positive words that describe Person #1, while Person #1 writes down each word, filling the sheet.
- Person #1 should write down what others are saying about them.
- Writing with your hand has a scientific connection to your brain.
- Person #1 should fully accept each word without questioning any of them.
- Repeat this process for each person in the group.

Once everyone has had a turn, take a few minutes of silence for each person to:

- Circle the words that appear on both sides of their paper.
- Place a star next to the words that give them the most expanded energy, or any other words they would like to discuss further.
- Engage in a group discussion where each participant shares what they learned or what they would like to know more about regarding themselves and others.
- Celebrate each other's unique strengths and qualities!

By understanding the impact of labels and consciously reshaping them, you break free from the constraints of low confidence and enjoy a more fulfilling and authentic life.


## 8. Seen, Heard, Spoken, & Written

In your daily life, words are ever-present. You encounter them throughout the day, and they have a profound impact on our thoughts and emotions. It's essential to recognize the significance of the words you see, hear, speak, and write, as they shape your outlook and self-image.

Imagine the power of words surrounding you in your everyday environment. From the signs on your walls to the interactions you have, words hold the ability to influence your thoughts and feelings. Have you ever caught yourself saying something your mother or father used to say? Your words are interconnected with your experiences, creating associations and meaning in your mind, regardless of the language you speak. You use words to express your thoughts, to communicate with others, and to evoke certain emotions.

Throughout the day, you likely encounter words that inspire, guide, and motivate you. Signs in your home offer messages of belief, welcome, or holiday cheer, while road signs and maps provide direction and create a sense of place. Consider the impact of a neighborhood sign like "Meadowbrook." Seeing the word itself conjures images of horses, meadows, and ponds, evoking feelings of serenity and peace. Words filter into your thoughts, shaping your emotions, and ultimately influencing the actions you take and the results you achieve, based on the images created in your mind as a result of the words that surround you daily.

Words have immense power when spoken. When you choose your words consciously, you may influence others, express yourself authentically, and inspire action. Sometimes you carefully consider your words, while at other times, they may slip out spontaneously. You may find yourself speaking more to clarify or rectify what you've said. This type of communication, recognized as overcompensation, occurs more often if you struggle with a lack of confidence driven by the feeling of being misunderstood; as a result, you may find yourself over explaining. In any case, each word you speak carries the potential to impact the actions taken or not taken, ultimately shaping daily experiences and outcomes.

Writing words is a way to preserve and solidify them. When you write, you memorialize your thoughts, engrave them into your consciousness, and even showcase them to the world. Writing allows you to share your chosen words, in the present and for future generations to come.

Now, let's conduct an experiment. Over the next three days, take note of the first three words you encounter each day. Pay attention to the words you hear from others or from your own inner voice. What are the first three words you speak and write? Notice any patterns or similarities among these words. How do they make you feel? Reflect on how they might have influenced your actions throughout the day.

After completing this exercise for three days, set aside time on the third day to review your findings. Consider how these words have affected you and think about how you may integrate them into your future days or choose to remove them from your days.

By becoming aware of the words in your daily life and intentionally selecting words that support and empower you, a positive outlook and self-image may be cultivated. Let us explore further how words may shape your experiences and how you harness their potential to boost our confidence and well-being.

Remember, the words you encounter and engage with daily have a profound impact on your thoughts, feelings, and actions. It's within your power to choose words that serve as a support system, providing encouragement, understanding, and validation. These words become the building blocks of a positive and confident mindset, helping you enjoy your experiences to the fullest.

# 9. Your Childhood

Words learned during your formative years have a lasting impact on your life.

As children, you absorb the words spoken around you and mimic the patterns and habits associated with those words. These early influences shape your growth and development, carrying over into adulthood.

For individuals with low confidence, experiences triggered by certain words or patterns of words evoke negative emotions like anxiety, self-consciousness, or inadequacy. These emotions overshadow the positive aspects of an experience, draining our energy and enthusiasm, and ultimately impacting our overall well-being.

Low confidence often accompanies self-limiting beliefs such as "I'm not good enough" or "I don't deserve happiness." These beliefs act as self-imposed barriers, restricting you from fully embracing positive experiences and pursuing your goals and aspirations. They become ingrained within you, affecting how you perceive yourself and interpret the world around you.

Consider the power of reframing negative beliefs into empowering ones. It's important to understand that current experiences are not fixed, and you have the power to change your beliefs and create a different reality. This begins with identifying the negative labels and self-talk you received during your childhood.

For instance, in my own experience, I grew up comparing myself to my sister, who excelled academically. Family members and others often described her as bright, quick-witted, and a good reader. As a result, I began to believe that I was not as smart as her. This belief became a label, a story I told myself, and it shaped my perception of my abilities and my life for many years.

One defining moment occurred when my grandfather jokingly referred to my sister as the "intelligent one," and me as the "dumb one." Although he intended it to be in good humor, those words had a significant impact on me. I internalized them and began to believe that school would be difficult for me. Despite the continued efforts made by my mother and sister to help me see myself differently, this label created a self-imposed barrier that hindered my confidence and limited my aspirations.

I was in my late 20s when I realized the truth: I am smart. I discovered success as a non-traditional college student, challenging the negative beliefs that had held me back. I shifted my mindset and began feeding my mind with empowering labels—"I am intelligent, capable, and worthy of success." This transformation empowered me to pursue my passions and embrace lifelong learning.

As Zig Ziglar wisely said, "You are where you are and what you are because of what has gone into your mind." The labels you internalize, in the form of words, shape your thinking, choices, and ultimately, your life. You do have the power to change the narrative by consciously choosing empowering words and thoughts.

Today, I invite you to reflect on your own childhood experiences and the labels or negative beliefs that may have influenced your confidence. Recognize that these beliefs are not absolute truths. Challenge them and reframe them into empowering statements. Affirm your intelligence, capabilities, and worthiness of success. By changing the words that enter your mind as an outward expression of yourself, you create a new inward reality of thoughts—one where you fully embrace positive experiences and pursue your goals with confidence.

Additionally, it's essential to be mindful of the labels unconsciously placed upon children, even with the best of intentions. Labels such as "shy," "difficult," "slow learner," "not good at...," "not as good as...," or "troublemaker" may inadvertently create limiting beliefs within the child, shaping their perception of themselves and their potential. It's crucial to remember that these labels do not define the essence of a child's being. Instead, let us focus on nurturing their unique qualities, encouraging their strengths, and celebrating their individuality. Let us extend this mindfulness to our interactions as adults as well, for labeling others is a form of judgment that hinders growth and self-belief. By refraining from putting labels on others, you create a space of acceptance, allowing each person to flourish in their own unique way.

In the next chapter, we explore practical strategies to identify and reframe negative beliefs, providing you with tools to cultivate a positive self-image and unlock your true potential. Remember, your journey towards confidence begins with your words, which you have the power to choose no matter where they show up.

## 10. Voices Inside Your Head

One of the most influential voices in our lives is the one inside our own heads. Have you ever stopped to wonder where that voice comes from? Is it your inner truth, the beliefs instilled by your parents, or the influence of those you have learned from or are afraid of?

The voices inside your head may often be challenging to recognize and acknowledge. They may be both motivational and critical, shaping your thoughts and perceptions. So, how do you begin to understand and recognize the words chosen by the voices inside your head?

These words, chosen by the voices within you, show up every single day. Even when you choose silence, the words inside your head may never cease. It is essential to grasp the significance of these inner voices, the words they choose, and the thoughts that generate them.

A few years ago, during a special training session, I had the privilege of learning from Mary Morrissey. In one exercise, she asked us to write down the things we say to ourselves most often, especially when contemplating something new or different.

As I engaged in this exercise, I anticipated writing down positive statements. However, as I put pen to paper, I realized that many of the words I used were not empowering. They were rather negative. Harsh phrases like "You're not good enough" or "That's too difficult for you" filled my list. These were the voices inside my head, holding me back and preventing me from taking action on things I would love to pursue. Up until that day, I had never invested any time to write down the voices that were in my head. I am forever grateful to Mary Morrissey for so many teachings, and especially for the lessons of that day.

The impact of the exercise became even more profound when I was instructed to speak these words to two strangers as my partners. As the couple, who happened to be an older couple and were both kind-hearted, repeated my self-deprecating statements louder and louder, I felt tears welling up. As I found the strength to respond with the words "I am more than that," a chuckle escaped, and I began to laugh at how absurd those statements truly were. They were not true; I was undoubtedly more than those limiting beliefs.

What I discovered about the voices inside my head was that once they were exposed—written down, spoken, and shared—I could understand the patterns and words I was choosing. These words had kept me from pursuing what I loved, and it was now my opportunity to break free from those patterns.

Now, I invite you to engage in this exercise. Write down the ten things you say most often to yourself when you want to try something new. Pay close attention to the voices in your head and the words chosen. And if you feel comfortable, share these statements with someone close to you. Have them stand behind you and repeat only your words, and as they do, you continue to loudly proclaim, "I am more than that," until you feel a sense of empowerment and have overcome those self-limiting voices.

Recommend each person take a turn with the same level of support. Remember, only the words the person writes about themselves are to be said in the exact way they have written them down.

While positive affirmations such as "You are beautiful," "You are strong," and "You are amazing" have their place, this exercise specifically targets the words you choose inside your head when attempting something new. Address those specific statements and challenge their validity. If you generally have a positive mindset and high energy, this exercise may not be necessary. However, if you find yourself engaging in self-doubt and negative self-talk, it is a powerful tool to experience.

By identifying and reframing the negative self-talk associated with a lack of confidence, you are empowered to break free from self-censorship and express yourself openly. You may overcome the fear of rejection and share your unique voice, contributing meaningfully to conversations and creative endeavors. It is within your power to reframe your inner dialogue and create a more empowering reality.

Remember, the voices inside your head do not define you. You are more than those self-limiting words. It's time to embrace your worth and let your authentic voice be heard.

## 11. Influence of Family & Friends: Shaping Word Choices

Have you ever considered how your family and friends influence the words you choose?

Have you ever considered the impact you have on each other by the words you each choose?

Perhaps you've noticed that you speak differently at work, using distinct tones and words, compared to when you're with your family. This difference in language may be influenced by the dynamics within your familial and social circles.

The influence of family and friends on our word choices is a significant aspect to explore. As you delve into the upcoming chapters, take a moment to reflect on what you learn, and consider sharing it with your loved ones.

When I began to pay attention to the power of words, I realized something intriguing during our family dinners. Sarcasm and teasing were prevalent, and while it seemed harmless, I discovered that the sarcasm often had a negative undertone, subtly putting down one another. It was unfortunate that I never noticed this earlier. Once I became aware, I implemented a new practice.

The practice was simple: For every negative comment, the person who said it had to replace what was said with two positive compliments to the person to whom the original negative comment was directed. Each person who received the initial sarcastic remark had to reciprocate by thanking the person and offering two compliments in return. This practice continued for several dinners, and gradually, the sarcastic tone dissipated from our family conversations.

It's truly amazing how quickly the choice of words within your circle of family and friends shifts once you become aware of the impact. By recognizing the influence of language and consciously choosing empowering words, you have the power to shape the dynamics within your relationships.

My wish for you is that as you engage with this book and explore the exercises included, your awareness is heightened. Through your own transformation, you have the opportunity to inspire and influence your family and friends to choose words that are more powerful, uplifting, and empowering.

Together, let's create a supportive environment where words are used to build one another up and foster deeper connections.

## 12. Investment in Time & Talents: Making a Difference

In this chapter, you have explored how words show up in every aspect of your life. You encounter words, hear them, speak them, and even rewrite them. They hold the power to influence how you invest your time and talents. By raising your awareness of the words around you and initiating change right where you are, you have the potential to transform yourself and make a positive impact on others.

If you are a teacher who has dedicated your time and talents to shaping the minds of children, you possess a unique opportunity. You may bring awareness to the words they choose and make a difference in their lives. The impact goes beyond the classroom, as they take these lessons home and share them with their families and friends.

As a leader in business, whether managing a team or an entire organization, you have the power to influence through the words you choose. Evaluate and shift the way you communicate with customers, employees, and shareholders. By leading with awareness and intention, you create a workplace environment where words uplift and inspire.

Even as a parent, sibling, aunt, uncle, or cousin, you hold the ability to shape the minds of the children and people you love the most. Your words carry weight and influence their outlook on life, their self-esteem, and their aspirations. Embrace this opportunity to make a positive impact and help them become the best versions of themselves.

As you continue reading and delve into the next section, you have the opportunity to learn how to uncover patterns within words. The chapters ahead focus on specific types of words and their meanings, opening your eyes to their impact in ways you may have never realized before.

As you embark on this transformative journey, it's important to have a guide who possesses deep expertise and a unique ability to help others open their minds to what is possible. Drawing on my years of experience and in-depth understanding of human behavior and mindset, I have honed my skills in identifying patterns and unlocking hidden potentials. Through the insights shared in this book, you will gain valuable tools and strategies to navigate life's challenges and create a future filled with purpose and fulfillment. Consider me your trusted companion on this path of personal growth and transformation, ready to support you in embracing your true potential and living a life you love.

Today is the day for transformation. By raising your awareness and actively applying what you learn in your day-to-day interactions, you have the power to make a profound difference in the lives of those around you and contribute to shaping a better world for future generations.

Embrace this journey and let the power of words guide you towards meaningful change.

# CHAPTER THREE

## Uncover Patterns

*"When you change the way you look at things,*
*the things you look at change."*
– Wayne Dyer

## 13. Absolute Certainty Implied

Words that imply absolute certainties have a profound impact on our personal growth and relationships. When you use words like "never," "always," or "it's impossible," you create a sense of finality and rigidity. These words limit potential, hinder ability to take risks, and restrict personal growth.

People with low confidence often find themselves trapped in the cycle of absolute certainties. The fear of failure or making mistakes prevents them from embracing new opportunities and stepping outside their comfort zones. The belief that they may "never" succeed or that things "always" go wrong, becomes deeply ingrained in their mindset. This mentality creates a self-imposed barrier, preventing them from fully experiencing life and hindering their personal development.

Furthermore, words implying absolute certainty affect your relationships with others. When you use such language, it creates a feeling of shutdown and a closed door. Interactions become limited, and true connections are hindered. In personal relationships, the inability to express needs, preferences, or boundaries, due to a fear of rejection or judgment, may lead to compromises that hinder one's ability to fully engage and enjoy experiences on their own terms.

In the context of business relationships and team dynamics, the impact of words implying absolute certainty is equally detrimental. Creativity and innovation are stifled when phrases like "It's always been done this way" or "We can never change" dominate the discourse. These words limit a team's ability to think outside the box, adapt to new challenges, and find innovative solutions. They create a culture of inaction and prevent progress towards achieving success and desired outcomes.

The power of words is undeniable. Words that imply absolute certainty breed inaction, close off possibilities, and limit personal and professional growth. They create a fixed mindset that keeps individuals stuck in their comfort zones, unable to explore new opportunities or take calculated risks. Breaking free from this pattern requires a conscious effort to challenge and reframe our language.

These three little magic words, "up until now," given to me by my mentor Mary Morrissey, are the first step in interrupting this type of pattern. They send a clear message that something is changing; that was then, and now.... As you progress through the next few sections, you'll discover how these magic words may be applied to shift various patterns. Keep them close to your heart and mind as you embark on this transformative journey through the following chapters and into your days.

For Example:

- Up until now, this has always happened to me. Beginning today, things are different because I ....
- Up until now, I've never been good with money. Now, things are different because I ....
- Up until now, things have been so hard. I am so happy and grateful now that things are easy.

In these examples, notice that you use the 3 magic words in front of the words used to describe the old experience. Then the next sentence contains what you would like the experience to be.

By developing awareness and implementing practical strategies, you overcome the limitations imposed by words that imply absolute certainty, and embrace a mindset of growth, possibility, and meaningful connections.

# 14. Famous Last Words

Famous last words are patterns that manifest when you feel a sense of giving up. These patterns often emerge when low confidence takes hold, making individuals more susceptible to setbacks and challenges. When faced with failures or rejections, many struggle to bounce back, perpetuating a cycle of negative experiences that further erode confidence. Building resilience becomes crucial for enjoying experiences fully and embracing new opportunities.

In the realm of low confidence, famous last words become significant barriers to personal growth, career advancement, meaningful relationships, and new adventures. Individuals with low confidence may find themselves uttering phrases like "I can't," "I've tried," or "I am," inadvertently limiting their potential and missing out on valuable opportunities. These words reflect fear, self-doubt, and a lack of belief in their own abilities.

The impact of these words extends beyond the individual and affects relationships with others. When famous last words are used, a sense of shutdown and closed doors prevails, hindering genuine connections. In personal relationships, the inability to express oneself due to fear or self-imposed limitations creates a barrier, preventing true emotional bonds from forming. In business relationships and team dynamics, the use of such words stifles creativity and innovation. When phrases like "It can't be done" or "We've tried everything" dominate the conversation, the potential for growth and success is severely limited.

Organizations suffer when famous last words permeate their culture. Inaction becomes the norm, hindering progress towards goals and desired outcomes. When individuals and teams believe that certain things are impossible or that they've exhausted all possibilities, they resign themselves to a state of stagnation.

Recognizing these patterns in yourself and others is essential. Famous last words serve as indicators of a giving-up mindset, where individuals believe they may no longer change their circumstances. Identifying these patterns allows you to challenge and begin to shift thoughts, leading to new possibilities and actions.

In the previous section, you discovered the power of three magic words: "up until now." These words serve as catalysts for change. By saying "up until now," you acknowledge that something is ending and create space for new beginnings. This shift in mindset and language opens up the possibility for fresh actions and ultimately changes results.

To recognize these patterns in others, listen for the famous last words they use. Phrases like "I've tried," "I can't," or "I can't anymore" indicate a pattern of giving up. By paying attention to these patterns, you may offer support, encouragement, and alternative perspectives.

As you continue reading and delve into the next section, you have the opportunity to uncover more connections between uncovering patterns of famous last words and the drivers of stress. Be engaged and open to the transformative journey ahead.

# 15. Stress Drivers

"Stress" words are a topic close to my heart, particularly as a woman leader in business. Throughout my 20-year corporate career, I was expected to be assertive and take control of situations. However, I soon realized that the words I had chosen unintentionally caused stress for myself, my teammates, my customers, and my loved ones. These words became a driving force, with the best intentions aiming to achieve desired results and yet often resulting in strained relationships and diminished joy and happiness in life.

So, what are these "stress" words that have such a powerful impact? Let's explore examples:

- "I have to …."
- "I must …."
- "I don't want …."
- "I want …."
- "I spent …."
- "I am trying …" or "I tried …."
- "I am going to get …."
- "I am making …."

Additionally, words like "always" and "never" may fall under the category of stress words, as they imply absolutes and leave no room for choices or flexibility.

Do you notice a common thread among these words? They all carry a sense of control or a desire to control situations. They often eliminate choices and options. For instance, when you say, "I have to see my family for the holidays," it feels forced and devoid of choice. A better approach would be to say, "I choose to see my family for the holidays." By shifting your language, acknowledging your choices, and embracing conscious decisions, you invite positive energy into your life.

It's crucial to recognize that "stress" words impact you and your relationships with others.

Furthermore, in business relationships and team dynamics, "stress" words create a sense of control and directive communication. They limit collaboration and inclusion, hindering the ability to arrive at the best outcomes for all. These words create stress for everyone involved, fostering a tense environment.

In organizations, stress words become barriers to success. They promote forced action, diminish creativity, and limit innovation. When "stress" words dominate the workplace, employees may feel trapped and unable to bring their full potential to the table. This stifles growth and hampers the collective progress of the team.

To counter the impact of "stress" words, there are simple yet powerful shifts in language to know about. Instead of using words like "spend" or "spent," replace them with "invest" or "invested." This change in perspective generates empowerment, creating a feeling that you have control over your resources—time and money. By choosing where to invest your time and money, you open yourself up to greater possibilities and experiences.

The decision to shift from using the words "spend" and "spent," which imply that my resources are gone without any return, to embracing the words "invest" and "investment," has had a profound impact on my life and the lives of my family members. This simple change in language has transformed our relationships and perceptions of time and money. By adopting the concept of investment, you unlock the ability to wholeheartedly enjoy the resources you possess, and experience genuine joy and fulfillment with every decision. It empowers conscious choices and recognizes the value and returns that come from investing resources wisely.

I encourage you to shift your own language over the next few days. Replace the word "spend" with "invest," and observe the difference in how you feel. Notice the positive shift in your energy and the expanded possibilities it creates. Let's embrace this change and share it with others, helping future generations find true joy and appreciation for the precious resources of time and money.

Together, we may break free from the constraints of stress words and create a more fulfilling and balanced life for ourselves and others.

# 16. Limiting Beliefs Dim the Light of Possibilities

### Understanding Limiting Beliefs

As you delve into this chapter on uncovering patterns, you'll notice a recurring theme: limiting beliefs. These deeply ingrained assumptions or perceptions constrain our thoughts, actions, and potential, hindering personal growth. Limiting beliefs stem from a variety of sources, including past experiences, societal influences, and self-imposed restrictions. They hold you back from reaching your full potential and undermine your confidence in what you may achieve.

### Common Limiting Beliefs

There are several common limiting beliefs that impact individuals in different areas of their lives:

**"I'm not good enough":** This belief involves feeling inadequate or unworthy, eroding self-confidence and deterring individuals from pursuing their goals or trying new things. It undermines their belief in their own abilities and potential.

**"I can't change":** This belief suggests that personal transformation or improvement is impossible. It fosters stagnation and hinders progress, as individuals accept their circumstances and feel powerless to create positive change in their lives.

**"Failure is unacceptable":** The fear of failure and viewing it as unacceptable leads to a reluctance to take risks or explore new opportunities. This belief may stem from the desire for success, and it ultimately limits growth and prevents individuals from reaching their full potential. Embracing a mindset that values learning and growth over a fear of failure, may lead to greater success and personal fulfillment.

**"Money is bad and I don't want or need it":** This belief associates financial success with negative attributes, perpetuating unconscious biases that believe people with money are unhappy or unloved. It leads to self-sabotage or avoidance of financial endeavors, preventing individuals from embracing their full financial potential and creating a positive relationship with money.

**"I don't deserve happiness":** This belief fosters feelings of guilt or unworthiness, hindering individuals from prioritizing their well-being and seeking fulfillment. It may be rooted in self-doubt and a lack of self-compassion, preventing individuals from embracing joy and taking steps towards their own happiness.

Limiting beliefs have their origins in a combination of personal experiences, cultural conditioning, and external influences. They may be shaped by childhood upbringing, societal norms, educational systems, and negative feedback from authority figures. Media portrayals, stereotypes, and societal biases contribute to the formation of these beliefs.

Limiting beliefs and unconscious bias are interconnected. Unconscious bias refers to automatic and unintentional preferences or prejudices we hold towards certain individuals or groups. These biases reinforce and perpetuate limiting beliefs by distorting our perceptions and judgments. They create a lens through which the world is viewed, and further entrench restrictive beliefs about ourselves and others.

Carrying limiting beliefs has a profound impact on individuals, organizations, teams, and families. Personally, these beliefs diminish self-confidence and hinder individuals from pursuing their passions, taking risks, or embracing personal growth opportunities. They create self-imposed barriers that impede progress and limit fulfillment.

In organizational settings, limiting beliefs undermine employee morale and performance. They stifle innovation, collaboration, and creativity, hindering growth and progress within teams and departments.

Within families, limiting beliefs may be passed down through generations, reinforcing patterns of self-doubt and inhibiting open-mindedness. They hinder healthy communication, create emotional barriers, and impede the development of supportive relationships.

Recognizing and challenging these limiting beliefs is essential for personal growth and self-empowerment. By replacing them with more empowering beliefs, individuals may unlock their potential, cultivate self-confidence, and create a more fulfilling life. Remember that these beliefs are not fixed truths; rather, they are perceptions that may be transformed with self-awareness, self-compassion, and a commitment to personal development.

Personally, I have experienced the detrimental effects of a limiting belief firsthand. For years, I carried the belief that "I don't deserve happiness," which held me back from fully embracing joy and experiencing fulfillment. This belief took root in my mind when I was 7 years old.

I vividly remember a day at my grandma's house with all of my family. It was a wonderful day filled with laughter and fun. On the way home, we stopped for ice cream, and I enjoyed every bite of my favorite vanilla soft-serve cone with a cherry hard coating. When I arrived home, my cousin Lori delivered devastating news—our beloved dog, Ginger, was missing.

Ginger had been a special companion to me, having been rescued from abuse and returned to my mom. We had formed a deep bond, and Ginger had even saved me from a hornet's nest a few weeks before. As we frantically searched for her, I blamed myself for having a good time that day. I believed that if I allowed myself to experience happiness, something bad would inevitably happen. I vividly recall those words echoing in my mind, though I never shared them with anyone else.

This self-imposed restriction on happiness stayed with me for decades, buried deep within my subconscious. It wasn't until I reached my 40s and embarked on a journey of personal development with the help of a coach that I confronted this limiting belief head-on.

The pivotal moment came unexpectedly, while I was shopping for shoes in a Macy's store. As I stacked up ten pairs of fun and vibrant shoes, I suddenly paused and asked myself, "What are you doing?" That question triggered a flood of emotions, and I realized that I had deprived myself of joy and fun for far too long. The memory of Ginger and my childhood decision resurfaced, and I understood the connection between that belief and my reluctance to indulge in happiness.

Sitting in the Macy's shoe department, I made a conscious decision to challenge and overcome this limiting belief. I committed to exploring what truly brings me joy and how I could incorporate more of it into my life. It was a life-changing moment, as I recognized that I deserved happiness. I began to prioritize experiences and activities that brought me genuine joy and fulfillment.

So, I encourage you to reflect on your own life and ask yourself: What limiting belief is dimming your light? What belief is holding you back from embracing your true potential and experiencing the joy and fulfillment you deserve? Take the time to uncover these beliefs, journal about them, and assess their impact on your life.

Interrupting these limiting beliefs requires the trying on of new ideas and possibilities. Challenge yourself with questions like "What if I could?" and "What if we could?" Open yourself up to the idea that change is possible, that success and happiness are within your reach. Replace those self-imposed restrictions with empowering beliefs that empower you to take bold steps and embrace a brighter future.

Remember, you have the power to reshape your beliefs and transform your life. By shedding the weight of limiting beliefs, you may illuminate your path, cultivate self-confidence, and create a life filled with joy, success, and meaningful connections.

## 17. Advertising Yourself as On Sale

How do you portray yourself on sale? It often involves downplaying accomplishments and/or compliments or rejecting them altogether.

Imagine receiving a compliment from a coworker about a beautiful sweater you're wearing. They express their admiration by saying, "I love your sweater!" In response, you say, "Oh, this old thing? I just picked it up at the local discount store and it is really old." In this scenario, you are discounting the compliment and minimizing the value of what you're wearing.

Why does someone advertise themselves as on sale? Perhaps it stems from a fear of standing out or a belief of not being good enough. There may be various reasons for putting yourself on sale, and one of the key indicators is in the patterns of words that advertise yourself as on sale, such as the use of discount words like "just" and phrases that reject compliments. These patterns have a significant impact on your self-confidence and how you perceive yourself in the eyes of others.

Here are examples of empowering language that may replace discount words and uplift self-confidence:

Instead of saying "just" or "only," use assertive language that emphasizes your capabilities and contributions. For example:

- "I have successfully completed multiple projects," instead of, "I have just completed a few projects."
- "I am able to handle this task with confidence," instead of, "I can only handle simple tasks."

Rather than using minimizing phrases like "I'm not an expert, but ...," express your knowledge and expertise with confidence. For instance:

- "I have extensive experience in this field," instead of, "I'm not an expert, but I know a little bit."
- "I have valuable insights to share," instead of, "I'm not sure if this is important, but ...."

Instead of deflecting compliments with phrases like, "It was nothing" or "I got lucky," accept and appreciate the recognition. For example:

- "Thank you! I worked hard on this project, and I'm proud of the results."
- "I appreciate your kind words. It means a lot to me that my efforts are recognized."

Replace self-deprecating statements with affirmations that highlight your strengths and abilities. For instance:

- "I am confident in my problem-solving skills," instead of, "I'm not very good at solving problems."
- "I have a unique perspective to offer," instead of, "I'm not sure if my ideas are valuable."

Use language that expresses belief in yourself and your potential for growth. For example:

- "I am continuously learning and improving," instead of, "I can't change; I'm stuck in my ways."
- "I am capable of achieving my goals," instead of, "I don't think I can accomplish much."

Remember, the words you choose shape your thoughts and beliefs. By consciously replacing discount words with empowering language, you uplift your self-confidence and cultivate a more positive and empowering mindset.

When you discount compliments or reject them altogether, you diminish your own value and worth. You undermine the positive feedback you receive from others and miss out on an opportunity to acknowledge your strengths and accomplishments. It's important to remember that receiving compliments graciously is not about arrogance or seeking validation; it's about recognizing and internalizing the positive aspects of yourself.

Receiving compliments plays a crucial role in building and nurturing self-confidence. When you genuinely accept compliments, you reinforce positive beliefs about yourself and your abilities. It's like fuel for your self-esteem, providing you with the motivation and encouragement to pursue your goals and dreams.

Moreover, embracing compliments aligns with the law of receiving. According to this law, the more open and receptive you are to receiving positive energy, the more abundance and positivity you attract into your life. By welcoming compliments with gratitude and appreciation, you create a positive feedback loop of self-confidence and personal growth.

It's time to let go of discount words and phrases that undermine your self-worth. Instead, practice receiving compliments gracefully, acknowledging your strengths, and embracing the power of positive feedback.

Remember, every compliment received is a testament to your unique qualities and contributions. By valuing and accepting compliments, you cultivate a stronger sense of self-confidence and open yourself up to a world of possibilities.

The simple act of saying "Thank you" and pausing to receive a compliment, holds tremendous power. First, it is a gift from the person giving it to you. Discounting or rejecting the compliment is like handing the gift back to the person. Second, it is an acknowledgment of your worth, a validation of your efforts, and a recognition of your strengths. When you graciously accept compliments, you honor the person giving you the gift of a compliment, and you honor yourself and the hard work you have put into your endeavors. It allows you to embrace your accomplishments and boosts your self-confidence. By stopping to receive compliments, you open yourself up to the positive energy and affirmations that come from others. It creates a cycle of positivity and appreciation, fostering a nurturing environment for personal growth and building meaningful connections. So, the next time someone pays you a compliment, embrace it with gratitude and let it shine a light on your self-worth.

## 18. The Stories You Tell Yourself

By now, you may have realized the immense power that words hold and the patterns they create in your life. These patterns, once uncovered, may be transformed to have a profound impact on your confidence and overall experiences. It all begins with the stories you tell yourself. These stories are more than idle words; they shape your reality and determine the course of your life.

Let's explore the origins of these stories and how they may be influenced by criticism, both from your own internal self-talk and/or from others. Sometimes, the negativity becomes so pervasive that it manifests as an abusive and dysfunctional relationship. It's important to acknowledge that these hurtful words are not a reflection of your true self. They are a reflection of the struggles, insecurities, and limitations of experiences of the person saying them. Remember, when someone else says these types of things to you, it is about their own inner battles and not you.

Changing your perspective is not a simple task—it requires time, patience, and self-compassion. Start by taking a moment to disconnect from your emotions and observe the situation from a different angle.

Shift your focus to yourself and recognize your worth, unique gifts, and positive impact on the world. Celebrate even the smallest strengths and give yourself credit for the person you've become. What are the qualities you appreciate about the person who speaks those negative words? Separate those aspects from the way they treat you.

Now, it's time to rewrite the narrative. Replace hurtful words with empowering ones. Challenge the negative self-talk by consciously choosing words of kindness, understanding, and appreciation for yourself. Speak to yourself as a friend would—with love, encouragement, and unwavering support.

Forgiveness plays a role in this journey. It is not an excuse for the hurtful words or to forget the pain they caused, rather a way to release their grip on your life and create space for healing. Practice the art of forgiveness and direct it towards your own well-being and growth. Repeat words of forgiveness and genuinely wish the person well who uttered those words on their own path of change.

Remember that you don't have to face this journey alone. Seek support from trusted friends, family, or professionals who can offer guidance and understanding. Surround yourself with positivity and uplifting influences that reinforce the new pattern of thoughts and words you're cultivating.

In a world where words have immense power, it is crucial to recognize the impact they have on us and others. The story I would like to share with you is a personal one, one that involves my nephew, Wilson, and a powerful lesson we learned together.

During a sleepover with my nieces and nephews, a teasing incident unfolded. One cousin started calling another cousin names, and it was a moment that called for intervention. Recognizing the significance of this opportunity, we gathered as a group to embark on a transformative exercise.

I handed each person a small index card, and we formed a circle. The rules were simple: Each person would receive a turn, and everyone else would share one positive word to describe them and then one for themselves. As each word was spoken, it was written down on the individual's card.

When it was Wilson's turn, he hesitated for a moment. With vulnerability in his eyes, he wrote down and circled a word that revealed his inner struggle at the time: "FAT." As he shared it with the group, laughter ensued, and the question that followed shifted the energy in the room.

I asked Wilson if being "FAT" was truly what he wanted to be. His response was a resounding "no." It was in that moment of honesty that we embarked on a journey of self-transformation. I invited Wilson to close his eyes and envision himself as he would love to be, to see the incredible potential within him.

With newfound clarity, Wilson then crossed out "FAT" on his card and replaced it with words that reflected his vision of himself: "strong and muscular." A smile formed on his face, and something shifted within him. Little did we know that this simple exercise would have a lasting impact on his life.

Years passed, and we reunited to open a time capsule that held the index cards. As we unfolded Wilson's card, we discovered that he had indeed grown into the person he had envisioned: a strong and muscular young man.

This story holds a profound lesson that echoes the wisdom of Wayne Dyer's quote, "As you change the way you look at things, what you look at changes."

In that moment, Wilson shifted his perspective and embraced a new story, one filled with strength and possibility. Through his unwavering belief in his potential, he manifested his vision and transformed his reality.

To Wilson, my nieces, my nephews, my children, my grandchildren and anyone reading this, I want you to know that you are all special. You possess incredible potential within you, and the words you choose to believe about yourself matters. Embrace the power of positive language and envision the extraordinary future that awaits you. As you change the way you look at yourself and the world around you, remember that the possibilities are endless.

May this story serve as a reminder that each of you has the power to shape your own narrative and become the incredible individuals you were meant to be. Embrace your unique qualities, envision your dreams, and let your words and beliefs propel you towards a future filled with joy, fulfillment, and endless possibilities.

Now it is your turn. Let's engage in an empowering exercise that will help reshape your story. Take out a journal or a piece of paper and dedicate time to self-reflection. Write down the words and phrases that you use to describe thoughts about yourself, things you would like to do, or even about your day. Notice the negative or disempowering words you find yourself repeating. Circle them as patterns, recognizing their presence in your internal dialogue.

Once you have identified these patterns, it's time for a transformative act. Cross out those negative words, liberating yourself from their hold. Then, in their place, write a new word or phrase that resonates with positive thoughts and self-belief. Let these empowering words become part of your vocabulary, affirming your worth and potential.

The act of writing out your words is a powerful tool in understanding the story you've been telling yourself. Crossing out negative patterns and replacing them with positive alternatives will change the way you look at things. So, it is for you, too, as Wayne Dyer wisely said, "As you change the way you look at things, what you look at changes."

Embrace this exercise as an opportunity for growth and transformation. Over time, you witness the profound impact it has on your self-perception, relationships, and overall well-being. Trust in the power of your words, for they have the potential to shape your reality and unlock a future filled with joy, self-love, and endless possibilities.

So, grab that pen and let your journey of self-discovery and empowerment begin. Rewrite your story, one word at a time, and watch as your world transforms. You have the strength within you to make this shift, and I wholeheartedly believe in you.

# CHAPTER FOUR

# Flip It, Flip It, Flip It

*"The best way to predict the future is to create it."*
**– Abraham Lincoln**

## 19. Say What You Want

In this section, dive into the power of saying what you want instead of focusing on what you don't want. It's probably common for you to invest a significant amount of time articulating what you don't want in your life, as a way to protect yourself from experiencing it. However, it may be rare that you invest the same amount of time and energy into expressing what you would love to have.

Think about it. If you plan a birthday party, you put in great time and effort to create lists with timelines, select the decorations, make a cake, and invite guests. The question is, how often do you invest the same level of time and detail in defining what you want your personal relationships to look like? How much time have you invested in outlining how you want your future to unfold?

For most of us, the answer is, "Not much." Often, you are living day by day, focusing on immediate concerns and going through the motions. Here is the crucial question: Have you ever taken 20 minutes to write down three pages describing what your ideal future looks like? Have you crafted a story about your life, envisioning the possibilities with confidence and empowered choices?

For many of us, sadly, the answer is, "Not since I was a young child." Remember those days when you effortlessly tapped into your imagination, when you were the master architect of your dreams? You would invest hours envisioning the life you desired, creating elaborate scenarios of your future self You would try on clothes from your imagination, build grand structures, or even pretend cardboard box rockets could transport you to extraordinary places. In those moments, you fully stepped into your dreams and believed in their possibility.

As we grow older, it's easy to lose touch with that inner child who knew no limits, who fearlessly explored the realms of imagination. The truth is, that child still resides within you, waiting to be awakened. That child knew how to dream without boundaries, to imagine a life filled with joy, success, and fulfillment.

Close your eyes and remember the excitement and wonder you felt as a child, as you imagined what your life could be. Reconnect with that boundless imagination and allow yourself to believe once again in the power of your dreams. You are capable of creating the life you envision, just as you did as a child.

It's time to dust off those dreams and give them the attention they deserve. Take a moment to imagine the work you would love to do, the home that reflects your unique style, the adventures you would embark on, the abundance you would enjoy, and the impact you would have on others. Allow yourself to feel the thrill of possibility, just as you did when you were a child.

Embrace your inner child's fearless spirit and let it guide you as you chart a path towards your dreams. Invest the same level of energy and imagination into designing your future as you did when you were young. Believe in the power of your dreams, for they hold the key to a life filled with joy and fulfillment.

The time has come to reconnect with your inner child and reignite the spark of imagination within you. Remember, you have the ability to create a reality that surpasses even your wildest childhood dreams. Embrace the journey ahead with open arms and let your imagination soar once more.

The key message here is to flip the narrative from talking about what you don't want, to speaking about what you do want. By investing your time, thoughts, and words into articulating your desires, you tap into the power of clarity and intention. It's a shift from control based on fear, to empowerment based on embracing your true desires.

Let's consider a few examples. If you find yourself saying, "I don't want to live alone anymore," notice how that statement focuses on what you don't want. Instead, flip it and say, "I would love to live with someone who embodies certain qualities, and together we may create a beautiful home and life." By shifting your energy towards what you truly want, you open yourself to new ideas, possibilities, and actions that align with your desires.

Similarly, if you're telling a child, "I don't want you to get dirty," you create a sense of control and stress. By flipping it and saying, "I would love for you to be clean, because we are going to Grandma's house," you communicate your preference without imposing control. You create an environment where the child feels empowered and understands the reason behind the request, such as going to Grandma's house.

These examples illustrate how flipping your words and focusing on what you want may lead to more open outcomes and better relationships. It's about letting go of control, embracing choice, and expressing your desires in a way that fosters connection and understanding.

If you tend to use words to describe what you do not want, or if you find yourself in a relationship with someone who primarily focuses on what they do not want when expressing their thoughts, it's essential to approach this with compassion and understanding. At the root of this pattern lies fear—a protective mechanism that stems from a deep sense of care and the desire for reassurance. To navigate this, it may be helpful to delve into the underlying fear and address it directly. Speak to that fear within yourself or within the other person; acknowledge its presence and offer assurance. Let it be known that you understand the concerns and that everything is going to be okay. By addressing the fear at its core, you create a space of empathy and support, allowing for a shift towards expressing what you truly want and embracing a more empowering dialogue.

Personally, I have come to view fear as a trusted companion on my journey. It represents the part of ourselves that genuinely cares about our well-being and wants to ensure our safety. Rather than disregarding or suppressing fear, I've learned that acknowledging its presence is crucial. Similar to a dear friend or a loved one, fear desires to provide protection and guidance. By taking a moment to pause, acknowledging fear's concerns, and assuring it of your clarity and confidence in your choices, you cultivate a harmonious relationship with fear. In doing so, fear transforms from a voice of control into a catalyst for personal growth. It challenges you to be intentional and precise in your thoughts and words, guiding you to step into your authentic power. Embracing fear as an ally allows you to transcend its grip and tap into a realm of unlimited possibilities and self-empowerment.

In the next section, it is time to explore the power of language, moving from stress-inducing words to empowering and fun expressions. For now, remember the lesson from the previous section: The stories you tell yourself shape your reality. By flipping the script and speaking about what you truly want, you unlock the potential for deeper connections in your relationships and a more fulfilling and abundant life.

# 20. Go From Push & Stress to Empowerment & Fun

Let's embark on a transformative journey, from the realm of stress and pressure to one of empowerment and enjoyment. How do you accomplish this?

Start by considering a common scenario: when a child is told they "have to" clean their room by the end of the day. Notice how the phrase "have to" removes choice and leaves little room for openness. How do you feel when you're told you have to do something? Are you truly happy and motivated, or do you experience feelings of frustration, anger, or even a desire to procrastinate? It's as if you're being forced into action, and we all know how well we thrive under pressure, right?

The truth is, you may effortlessly shift from the push and stress of "have to," to a more empowering approach. Instead of imposing, choose to say, "I would love to," or ask someone, "Would you be willing to clean your room before the end of the day?" By invoking the power of choice, you grant autonomy and relinquish control. You accept that whether the room gets cleaned or not is ultimately up to them, and that's okay.

More often than not, when given the choice, people respond positively and willingly. You'll be amazed at how frequently they accomplish the task and do so with a sense of satisfaction. Meanwhile, you may relax and enjoy the process, knowing that you have been open to their decision. Let's apply this approach to yourself.

Consider this example: "I have to make a cake for the party." If you keep repeating to yourself all week, "I have to, I have to, I have to," you'll begin to feel compelled and devoid of choice. Slowly, all the fun associated with baking the cake is sucked out. So, how do you maintain a sense of empowerment and fun? You reframe it by saying, "I am choosing to make a cake for my friend's birthday party." By emphasizing the power of choice, you lighten the burden and become much more willing to go to the store, gather the ingredients, and embrace the process with joy. You feel empowered because you made the conscious decision to make the cake, and that fills you with happiness.

## 21. Begin With the Opposite to Attract Positive Results

In the beginning, it is important to deliberately choose the exact opposite of the words that you would normally choose in order to attract positive results. By becoming aware of the words you see, hear, speak, and write, and by uncovering patterns, you shift your focus to what you would love, instead of what may seem like a burden. As you do this, you gradually observe a transformation in your thoughts and feelings, as they become more positive and uplifting. This shift brings about an increase in energy, propelling you to take inspired actions that align with your dreams and aspirations. Consequently, you start to attract positive results into your life.

To help you embark on this transformative journey, here are examples to guide you along the way and support you in choosing the opposite words to attract positive results:

| Force Words = Push & Stress | Empowerment Words = Vision & Fun |
|---|---|
| I have to … | I would love to … |
| I must … | I am happy to … |
| I don't want … (easy to identify) | I would like … (focus on the desire) |
| I am trying or I try … | I am taking an action, or I take actions to … |
| I always … | I am able to … |
| I never … | This is new … |
| I am going to get … | I would love … |
| I spent x on … | I invested x in … |

## 22. Language Observations

In the journey of life, you begin as a baby, observing the language that surrounds you. Your first language is shaped by the words spoken by whomever raised you. English, Spanish, or any other language—these are the building blocks that form the foundation of your journey. Today, as you explore the distinction between negative and empowering words, you unlock the power to achieve positive outcomes. By observing language in this way, you embark on a path of learning a new language—the language of empowerment.

For me, this journey has become a habit—a habit of carefully observing my own words in writing, speaking, and even listening. It may go unnoticed by many, yet I often find myself correcting the language choices of those around me, which is key to the work I do with my clients. Language observations have become my way of life, inspired by the clients I work with. Through this book, my intention is to share these observations with the world, so that you may transform your results and live the life of your dreams, becoming the person you were always meant to be.

How did I begin this practice of language observations? It started with the words I encountered within the walls of my own home. I removed signs that carried negative connotations, even if they were meant to be sarcastic or humorous. The signs you see upon waking up, as mentioned in Chapter three, provide an excellent starting point. By changing those initial words and replacing them with ones that bear positive, motivational, and loving words, I set the tone for my day.

Next, I became attuned to the language used by others. I listened carefully and then consciously shifted my own language or rephrased what I heard, in a way that aligned with the positive language to be explored in these chapters. I began to see and hear things differently. Whenever I caught myself using negative connotations or limiting words, I corrected them. I rephrased my sentences in a more positive manner, establishing a new habit—one that I strive to embody every day. Is it perfect? No. Generations of conditioning with negative or protective words still have their presence, I started somewhere. The changes I made for myself, I extended to my family, teammates, clients, and to all those dear to me. And hopefully, this helps you, the reader, and anyone you choose to share this wisdom with.

Writing has become one of the most powerful tools in adjusting my language habits. When writing, I easily began to spot my words on the page or screen. It gave me the opportunity to reflect and review my words and delete and rewrite them if needed. This exercise was immensely helpful in getting started. While I may have invested more time to compose texts and emails, what I learned was priceless. I discovered that my writing often carried stress and force, imposing my own opinions on others. Stepping back, observing, and considering if the words I chose were truly uplifting to me and those receiving my message, became a transformative practice.

In observing language, you uncover your weaknesses and gain the opportunity to leverage them for growth. By emotionally connecting with the power of words, you harness their strength and transform your communication, thoughts, and ultimately, your life.

## 23. Choose Positive

Choose the path of positivity. Embrace the power of positive words in every opportunity that presents itself. By opting for words that expand and uplift, you'll witness the incredible impact they have on your day and everyone around you.

Let's delve into the significance of removing the word "but" from your vocabulary. Consider how this simple switch may alter the entire meaning of a sentence. The word "but" automatically sets the stage for something negative. It's like putting up a roadblock that hinders progress and creates a sense of limitation.

Now, let's explore a different example, one that resonates deeply in our relationships. Imagine you're having a conversation with a loved one, and they share their dreams and aspirations. They express their desire to pursue a new career path that aligns with their passion. If you respond with, "That sounds great, but it's going to be difficult to find a job in that field," you unintentionally dampen their enthusiasm and introduce doubt into their journey. The conversation becomes a battle between their dreams and the challenges ahead.

Instead, let's consider an alternative approach, one that nurtures support and inspiration. What if you respond with, "That sounds great, and I believe in you. Let's explore together how to find job opportunities to take you in the direction of your dreams becoming a reality." By replacing "but" with "and," you acknowledge their aspirations while acknowledging the need to address potential obstacles in job opportunities. This creates an environment of encouragement, collaboration, and unwavering belief in their abilities.

Removing the word "but" from your vocabulary opens the door to more harmonious interactions and fosters a mindset of collaboration and understanding. It allows for the exploration of possibilities rather than imposing limitations. Embrace the idea of "flipping it," from "but" to "and," which works almost every time. Try it on! You may even consider omitting the word "but" altogether when transitioning between thoughts. Instead of placing a comma before "but," insert a period and STOP. Pause and ask yourself, are the words following "but" truly necessary? Perhaps not. If they aren't, then simply stop and end the sentence. If they are important, consider starting a fresh new sentence or replacing the "but" with "and." By doing so, you'll uncover the transformative power of positive language, creating a more expansive and joyful experience for yourself and those around you.

## 24. How to Begin Helping Others

When it comes to supporting others in their word choices and fostering a positive mindset, there are several simple yet impactful ways to respond. Let me share a personal story that exemplifies this.

Earlier this year, I was messaging with my 11-year-old grandson, Braylon, discussing his favorite pizza place. He excitedly told me, "Finally found a place where the cheese doesn't fall off!" Now, if you analyze his statement, it becomes apparent that he was focused on what he didn't want—the cheese falling off—and trying to control it. This approach may chip away at the joy and love for pizza, creating unnecessary stress.

However, there is another way to respond that may help others reframe their words in a more positive manner. In my interaction with Braylon, I chose to say, "That's awesome! So glad you found a place where the cheese stays on." By shifting the focus to what he wanted—the cheese staying on—you create a sense of freedom and excitement. This simple change in language empowers him and encourages a more positive outlook.

This example illustrates one of the ways you may assist others in their word choices. Another opportunity arises when someone asks you to review their work, such as a child or student writing a paper, or a teammate's presentation. This is a perfect moment to help them with positive word choices. By saying the same thing with different words that evoke different thoughts and emotions, you make a profound impact.

In the next chapter, there are fun ways to apply these principles, both for yourself and when helping others. Remember, by consciously choosing positive language, you uplift those around you and contribute to a more joyful and empowering environment.

# CHAPTER FIVE

# Tips & Tricks to Start the Change

*"We have the opportunity to live in joy."*
**– Mary Morrissey**

## 25. Create a New Game

The best way to learn is often through enjoyable and engaging activities. As you review these chapters and delve into these principles, you might initially find it challenging to make the shift, and you may feel overwhelmed by the task of using more positive words, especially if you're accustomed to your current language habits.

I have discovered that one of the most effective ways to support my clients in creating positive change is by introducing new games and exercises. Let me share a couple of ideas that you may incorporate into your journey, as a single player or with a group of players:

- **Word Swap:** Select a paragraph or a piece of writing and ask the players to identify any negative words or phrases. Once they've identified them, encourage them to replace those negative words with positive ones. This exercise helps train the mind to become more aware of negative language patterns and actively seek positive alternatives.

- **Positive Word Associations:** Provide the players with a list of negative words and ask them to come up with positive word associations for each one. For example, if the negative word is "failure," the positive word association could be "growth" or "learning opportunity." This game helps reframe negative concepts into positive ones and expands their positive vocabulary.

- **Sentence Rewrites:** Give the players a sentence containing negative language and ask them to rewrite it using positive language. For instance, if the sentence is, "I can't do it," they may rewrite it as, "I am capable of achieving it." This exercise encourages them to consciously rephrase negative statements into positive affirmations.

- **Word Substitutions:** Provide a list of common negative words and phrases, such as "can't," "impossible," or "I don't know," and challenge the player to come up with alternative words or phrases that convey positivity and possibility. This game helps them become more mindful of their word choices and encourages creative thinking.

- **Positive Word Scavenger Hunt:** Ask the player to go through their environment, whether it's a book, magazine, or online articles, and find positive words or phrases. They may create a list or collect examples that resonate with them. This activity helps them actively seek out positive language and expands their awareness of its presence in different contexts.

Feel free to adapt these ideas or create your own word games that resonate with you. The aim is to create an enjoyable and engaging learning process. Remember, incorporating more positive language, even with simple games, has a profound impact on your mindset and overall well-being. Embrace the journey and have fun exploring the transformative power of words!

## 26. Listen to What You Listen To

Listening is a powerful tool that shapes your perception of the world around you. From the moment you are born, hearing becomes one of your primary modes of intake. It's through listening that you absorb the words and messages that influence your thoughts, feelings, and actions. Have you ever considered the impact of the words you hear?

When you listen to words filled with positivity and empowerment, you are more likely to be motivated and take action. These are the words that truly help you achieve the results you desire. Positive words uplift you, while empowering words propel you forward on your journey. It's important to distinguish between positive words and words that empower you to take action, as they do hold different levels of influence.

In the game of life, just like in sports, the words we choose hold tremendous power, especially for those who grapple with perfectionism. Picture this: You're on the field, and you hear the coach's voice booming, "Shoot it!" But let's pause and think about this. Does "shoot it" really encompass the essence of finishing the shot and scoring that goal you've been dreaming of? My sister, Carrie Hanna, has dedicated her life to sports; and being a soccer coach, she has a gem of wisdom she imparts to her players: "Finish it." These two simple words carry the weight of determination, urging you to go beyond just taking a shot, and instead focus on achieving that ultimate goal.

Now, let's explore how words impact players' minds and emotions. Imagine a coach advising, "Don't be too perfect." In the pursuit of avoiding perfection, the player feels the weight of your worry, and maybe the player also believes they struggle with perfectionism; and suddenly, their every move becomes strained with stress and anxiety. In those critical moments of the game, the focus shifts from finishing the shot, to the relentless pursuit of flawlessness, ultimately leading to missed opportunities.

In life, caution is crucial when it comes to negative words in your conversations or self-talk. Just like the universe, the mind often overlooks the word "don't," and your focus unwittingly shifts to what you want to avoid. Instead, let's embrace words that inspire and uplift, urging you to keep going and to persevere. By internalizing words like "finish it," you empower yourself to move towards the desired outcome with determination and purpose.

So, whether you're on the field or navigating the challenges of life, remember the profound impact of the words you choose. Together, let's rewrite the script, replacing doubt with encouragement and transforming our pursuits into triumphant victories.

When selecting motivational or inspirational content to listen to, choose messages that guide you on what to do and inspire positive action and upward mobility. Be mindful of the language patterns and stress-inducing words discussed earlier, and consciously seek out conversations and media that uplift and inspire you.

Moreover, be aware of the people you surround yourself with and the conversations you engage in. If you find yourself in a conversation where someone speaks negatively about another person, you have the power to shift the tone. Introduce something positive about the person being discussed; find one thing you appreciate or admire. This shift in focus may either prompt the person to stop their negative talk or lead them to acknowledge positive aspects as well. Over time, you'll notice a shift in the conversations you attract, as people become less likely to involve you in negative discussions.

Remember, you have the power to choose what you listen to. Be intentional in selecting music, television shows, and conversations that align with your desire for positivity and empowerment. What you listen to becomes the nourishment for your mind, shaping your thoughts, feelings, and ultimately, your actions and results. Be mindful of this power and choose wisely.

# 27. See What You See

Seeing is more than a visual experience; it's an opportunity to absorb messages that shape our thoughts and feelings. Earlier, there was mention of the impact of inspirational signs and messages that surround you. These visual cues enter your mind and contribute to the formation of your thoughts and subsequent emotions. By now, you understand the profound connection between what you see and how it influences your inner world.

Let's explore another realm, where seeing plays a crucial role—the theater of your mind. When you sit in silence and reflect, it's common to visualize images. However, these images are often associated with words that interrupt or change your thought patterns. It's essential to recognize this process and take conscious control over what you see in your mind's eye. By actively changing the images and the corresponding words, you shape your internal narrative and promote positive thinking.

Beyond the theater of the mind, pay attention to what you see in your external environment. Take the time to notice what you see in your emails, text messages, and social media feeds. Be mindful and honest with yourself about the messages that enter your awareness. Remember that even a simple change in the words you encounter makes a significant difference in your mindset. In a world where you are constantly bombarded with diverse messages, being aware and deliberate about what you choose to see becomes increasingly important.

If you're a parent, you have a unique opportunity to shape the visual experiences of your children. Mindfully consider the words they see, the messaging they are exposed to, and take deliberate steps to shift their environment towards positivity. By doing so, you contribute to the transformation of language for generations to come.

In essence, seeing goes beyond mere observation—it becomes a gateway to transforming your inner and outer world. Take the time to notice what you see, make intentional changes, and allow the power of positive language to reshape your experiences.

## 28. The Power of Writing

When you speak, see, and hear, acknowledge that you are constantly exposed to external influences, and you may not always have complete control over the messages you interact and respond to. However, writing is different. When you write, you consciously choose the words you put down, whether it's in a text, email, note, or on paper. It becomes a deliberate act of selecting the language you choose to use.

There is significant power and value in writing: It allows you to see your thoughts in tangible form, whether it's on paper or in a digital format. When you write, you clearly see the patterns of your thoughts through the words you choose. It becomes evident when we observe the contrast, the difference between using positive and negative words. It becomes clear, like black and white, that the power lies in our choice of language. You may directly observe your patterns and make conscious changes through writing.

If there is a word that consistently appears in your writing, be certain that word is influencing how you speak and think on a daily basis, even if it's on a subconscious level. It reveals itself to you on paper, offering a tremendous opportunity for growth.

What is that opportunity?

It's the exercise of crossing it out, to put a giant X through it. Whether it's in your journal or a review journal, this exercise is immensely valuable. Set aside time every day. For example, if you dedicate 15–20 minutes to journal, with a goal to write three pages, during this time, you may truly observe your word patterns. If there are words you no longer wish to use or see, cross them out and rewrite the narrative in the way you desire. Create the language you would love to read and witness it manifesting.

Writing is truly one of the greatest gifts you have. It provides you with a way to understand and explore your thoughts through the words that show up in front of you. If you're eager to learn more about this exceptional practice, there is more to discover in the next section.

## 29. Snip It

As you embark on your writing journey, it's important to create space and separate the unnecessary words from your expression. These unnecessary words, the ones that tend to sneak in and sabotage your message, are what I call self-sabotage.

My mentor, Pat Slowey, used to say to me quite often, "Stop picking the fly sh***t out of the pepper." Yes, it is funny. One of the best ways to learn is through humor. Plus, this always made me think of my grandmother's kitchen table on the farm. It was hard to discern the fly shit from the pepper, and I knew that, so I understood what he was saying conceptually. At the time, I thought he did not want all the details that were so important to understand. As all mentors do when they patiently repeat messages, they somehow know the seed of the lesson is planted, and over time, it grows. I realize now, his intention was to help me focus on the bigger picture and let go of overwhelming details that were creating confusion and distracting from my core message.

Let me share another personal experience that resonates with this struggle. There was a point in my career where I had a successful interview, and as I wrote my thank-you email to the hiring manager, I added a phrase that diminished my confidence. I said, "Even if I don't get the role, it is still an honor to be a part of the team." Deep down, I truly desired the promotion, and yet fear and self-doubt crept in. Those additional words I added carried the weight of what I didn't want. They were unnecessary and self-sabotaging. I did not receive the promotion; and yes, I remained as part of the team for several years.

It's not uncommon to fill communications with excessive words that serve no purpose. In fact, these extra words often carry a negative connotation. So, I ask myself, when I write emails or respond in conversations, may I simply stop at "thank you" or "you're welcome?" Do I need to add anything else? The answer is likely no. Expressing genuine gratitude, "thank you" or "you're welcome," and acknowledging the impact the other person had, is more than enough. It allows them to receive gratitude for the gift of the compliment without any distractions.

My sincere advice to you is to simplify your words and eliminate unnecessary additions. Unnecessary words only create friction and undermine the value you bring to the situation. Let your message stand confidently and authentically, free from self-sabotage. Remember, less is often more impactful.

I have a special tool to share with you: "Snip it!"

There is a common struggle when it comes to communication: the fear of not being heard and the tendency to overcompensate as a result of lower confidence. It's a challenge that many of us face, and I have a powerful tool that may help overcome it: "Snip it."

Imagine taking a pair of scissors in your hand and visualizing the act of snipping away unnecessary words. This tool, the metaphorical scissors, allows you to cut through the clutter and create clear messages that are easily understood. By snipping those unnecessary words, you create space for your authentic voice to shine through.

The impact of "snip it" goes beyond improving communication. It's a symbolic gesture of letting go. As you snip away the extra words, you may find it helpful to use those same scissors to let go of the past and the situations and circumstances out of your control. As you visualize the scissors cutting through the unnecessary clutter in your communication, you may choose to release the burdens that may hold you back.

Snipping away those unnecessary words is not only a practical tool for clear communication; it's also a powerful act of self-empowerment. It allows you to let go of fears and insecurities, freeing yourself to express your thoughts and ideas confidently. As you embrace the "snip it" approach, you may find that your messages become more impactful, and you gain a renewed sense of confidence in your communication.

So, grab your metaphorical scissors and embrace the power of "snip it." Cut away the unnecessary words, let go of the past, and watch as your authentic voice shines through, ensuring that you are heard and understood.

## 30. Practice, Practice, Practice

Throughout my personal development journey, I've come across various pieces of information and insights. However, I believe that the code I've developed for positive words in this book is truly something special. It has the power to transform personal self-talk and communications with others, opening minds to expansive thoughts, feelings, actions, and ultimately, results.

During personal development exercises to understand the voices in my head, I made an interesting observation. I realized these voices often echoed words that others had said to me at some point, or things I had overheard. This became further evident when I did a self-talk exercise with my son, Aarik. As he openly shared his negative self-talk, I recognized that some of the words and phrases he used were words I had spoken to him over the years. While he may not have realized it, I definitely did. It was a profound realization that the words each of us use have a lasting impact on others, especially our loved ones.

It was never my intention for the words I used out of anger or frustration to become his self-talk. It helped me realize the words used in moments of anger and frustration are often learned and become default responses when those emotions arise. This led me to contemplate the possibility of replacing those words with empowering ones whenever frustration or anger enters my mind. Moreover, I wondered if I could help others do the same, to help shape a future where generations to come embrace empowering words as their default language.

The worldview of word choice impact is significant. The words you choose shape your perceptions, beliefs, and interactions with the world. They may inspire and uplift, or they may harm and limit. By becoming aware of the power of your words and actively practicing positive language, you all have the opportunity to create a positive ripple effect in your own life and in the lives of those around you. Imagine a world where words consistently empower, encourage, and elevate one another.

In the following chapters, there are more practical tools, exercises, and techniques to help you refine your word choice and cultivate a language that uplifts and inspires. Through practice, repetition, and conscious awareness, you may reshape your inner dialogue and external communication, fostering a more positive and empowering environment for yourself and others.

A special thank you to you for joining me on this personal development journey. The power of language and the influence it has on our thoughts, emotions, and interactions is a significant aspect of personal growth and development. By exploring this topic in depth and exploring the offerings of practical tools and insights, you have given me the opportunity to help the world become more conscious of language choices and transform communication patterns.

# CHAPTER SIX

## Strengthen Your Choices

*"The difference between the right word and almost the right word is the difference between lightning and a lightning bug."*
– Mark Twain

## 31. The Way You Do One Thing Is the Way You Do Everything

You undoubtedly notice that the way you approach one aspect of your life often reflects how you approach everything else. Take, for example, the simple act of waking up in the morning. If you find yourself hitting the snooze button, procrastinating the inevitable, it's likely that this tendency to delay extends to other areas of your life—other decisions, opportunities, and commitments.

Words matter, as Mark Twain once astutely observed: "The difference between the right word and the almost right word is the difference between lightning and a lightning bug." Reflecting on Twain's words, you may realize that the choice of words holds immense power. It may be the difference between a small flicker and a magnificent burst of inspiration. The words you select have the ability to ignite a fire within you, propelling you towards the fulfillment of your desires.

When I ponder Twain's quote, I contemplate its meaning and its implications for my own life. It reminds me that the words I choose today have the potential to shape the opportunities and outcomes that await me in the future. If I allow my words to be laden with negativity, doubt, or self-sabotage, I inadvertently close doors and limit my potential. On the other hand, by consciously selecting words that empower, inspire, and uplift, I open myself to a world of endless possibilities and embrace the radiant path of growth and success.

By understanding the profound impact of your word choices, you delve deeper into the practice of strengthening your choices. Where does the strength of your choices come from? While personal journeys and life experiences shape us, this book isn't solely an autobiography of my own struggles and triumphs. Rather, it is an exploration of words, their relevance in today's world, and the transformative power they hold.

You are living in a time where new generations are driven by a pursuit of quality of life, recognition for their true selves, and the belief that anything is possible. They refuse to be restricted by circumstances or conditions. This shift in perspective presents a unique opportunity to examine how our words impact our lives and the lives of those around you.

Reflecting on the lessons you've learned from previous generations, you may acknowledge the progress made, yet recognize the hesitations, doubts, and uncertainties that accompanied your journeys. Today, as you contemplate the significance of words, you may find yourself in a pivotal moment. The words you've used in the past may have hindered your progress or fostered unhealthy competition and strife. Now is the time to break free from those patterns and embrace a new way of speaking, a new way of relating to one another—a language rooted in empowerment, unity, and growth.

By consciously choosing your words, you have the power to uplift yourself and others, to reshape your perspectives, and to ignite transformative change. This book aims to provide you with the tools, insights, and guidance to embrace the world-altering potential of your language. Together, let us embark on this journey of self-discovery and linguistic transformation, as we unlock the extraordinary power of our words and shape a brighter future for generations to come.

Remember, the way you do one thing is indeed the way you do everything.

The following sections explore even more practical strategies and exercises to strengthen your word choices and enhance your communication skills, empowering you to create a positive impact in all areas of your life.

## 32. Begin to Eliminate Static & Interference

In our journey to strengthen your choices and transform the way you communicate, it is crucial to address the issue of static and interference that often disrupts the clarity and impact of your words. You may encounter moments when your confidence wavers, causing you to rely on filler words and phrases that dilute the power of your message. However, by consciously eliminating these fillers, you may deliver clear and concise messages that resonate deeply with others.

Filler words, such as "um," "like," "you know," and "uh," may tend to sneak their way into your speech patterns when you're uncertain or searching for the right words. While they may serve as temporary crutches, they create unnecessary noise and distractions, hindering effective communication. They dilute the strength of our message and leave listeners struggling to grasp our intended meaning.

In your everyday conversations, you may often find yourself relying on words like "actually" and "very" to emphasize or reinforce your statements. However, these words inadvertently introduce static and interference into your communications. For instance, when someone says, "I'm actually very happy about this opportunity," the excessive use of "actually" and "very" dilutes the impact of their happiness, creating a sense of uncertainty. By eliminating these words and simply stating, "I'm happy about this opportunity," the message becomes clearer and more authentic, allowing the true depth of the emotion to shine through. Strive for clarity and precision in your words, reducing unnecessary noise and enhancing the power of your communication.

So, how may you begin to eliminate these fillers and cultivate a more intentional and impactful way of speaking? Here are a few strategies to consider:

- **Awareness:** The first step in overcoming any challenge is to become aware of it. Pay close attention to your speech patterns and take note of the filler words you frequently use. Listen to recordings of your conversations or presentations to identify patterns and areas for improvement. By acknowledging the presence of filler words in your speech, you are already on the path to eliminating them.

- **Pause and Reflect:** Instead of resorting to fillers during moments of uncertainty, embrace the power of silence. Pause and take a breath, allowing yourself time to gather your thoughts. Use this pause as an opportunity to formulate a clear and concise response. Remember, it's okay to take a moment to think before speaking.

- **Practice Active Listening:** Actively listening to others may help you become more mindful of your own speech patterns. Pay attention to how others communicate, particularly those who speak with clarity and precision. Observe how they structure their sentences, express their ideas, and convey confidence. By immersing yourself in effective communication examples, you may learn to mirror and adopt those practices.

- **Replace Fillers with Purposeful Language:** Train yourself to substitute filler words with purposeful language. Instead of saying "um" or "like," pause and choose words that accurately convey your thoughts. Embrace concise and confident statements that eliminate the need for fillers. The more you practice this substitution, the more natural and fluid your speech becomes.

- **Visualization and Affirmation:** Visualize yourself delivering clear and considerate messages without relying on fillers. Imagine yourself speaking with confidence and connecting effortlessly with your audience. Reinforce this mental image with positive affirmations. Repeat phrases such as, "I speak with clarity and conviction," or "My words resonate powerfully," to reaffirm your commitment to eliminating fillers.

Remember, the process of eliminating fillers requires patience and practice. It may take time to break old habits and establish new ones. Be kind to yourself throughout this journey, celebrating each victory along the way.

As you consciously work towards eliminating static and interference from your words, you experience a profound shift in how you communicate. Your messages become clearer, your presence more impactful, and your connections with others deeper and more authentic. Embrace this opportunity to craft your words deliberately and leave a lasting impression with your communication prowess.

In the following sections, we explore additional techniques and exercises to further enhance your communication skills, empowering you to create meaningful connections and inspire positive change through your words.

## 33. Recognize Names Matter

The power of words cannot be underestimated, and they may have a significant impact on our well-being and sense of self. As an individual who personally has grown up using two different first names and has had three different last names, I have personally experienced how it feels when there is confusion on the name used when addressing me directly or speaking about me.

In your interactions with others, one of the most powerful and personal aspects of communication is the use of names. The simple act of addressing someone by their individual personal name has a profound impact on how they feel and perceive themselves. It shows respect, acknowledgement, and creates a sense of connection. On the other hand, mispronouncing or forgetting someone's name creates feelings of disconnection, insignificance, and even offense.

To truly harness the power of names, it's essential to prioritize accuracy and attentiveness. Here are tips to help you improve in this area:

- **Actively listen:** When you meet someone for the first time, pay close attention to their name. Listen carefully to the pronunciation and commit it to memory. Avoid distractions and make a conscious effort to show genuine interest in the person you are speaking with.

- **Repeat and clarify:** If you're unsure about the pronunciation or spelling of someone's name, don't hesitate to ask for clarification. It's better to take a moment to ensure accuracy than to make assumptions. Repeat their name back to them to confirm that you have understood it correctly.

- **Practice, practice, practice:** If you struggle with remembering names, practice is key. Make a conscious effort to use people's names when you address them in conversations. Write down names and review them later to reinforce your memory. The more you practice, the better you become at recalling and using names effortlessly.

- **Apologize and correct mistakes:** If you happen to mispronounce or forget someone's name, take responsibility for your error and apologize sincerely. Don't be afraid to ask for their name again; make a genuine effort to get it right moving forward. Taking this initiative shows respect and demonstrates your commitment to valuing them as an individual.

Remember, names hold significance and are a fundamental part of a person's identity. By recognizing the importance of names and making a conscious effort to use them correctly, you foster stronger connections, build trust, and demonstrate your genuine care for others.

It is worth noting that while some instances may be unintentional or due to oversight, repeated use of the wrong name may be seen as a lack of respect or disregard for the individual's identity.

As you practice using names with intention and accuracy, you find that your interactions become more meaningful, and the impact of your words and presence becomes amplified.

Using the correct name, whether it's your own or your team's, is an essential aspect of respectful and inclusive communication. Here's why using the correct name matters:

- **Identity and respect:** Our names are an integral part of our identity. When someone consistently uses the wrong name, it may feel dismissive, disrespectful, and even dehumanizing. Using the correct name demonstrates that the person acknowledges and respects your individuality and autonomy.

- **Recognition and validation:** Using the correct name acknowledges your existence and validates your presence. It affirms that you are seen, heard, and valued as an individual. When your name is consistently disregarded or replaced, it may lead to feelings of insignificance, erasure, and being overlooked.

- **Professionalism and credibility:** In a professional setting, using the correct name is crucial for maintaining professionalism and credibility. It shows attention to detail, an understanding of proper business etiquette, and a willingness to establish positive working relationships. Conversely, consistently using the wrong name may undermine your professional image and credibility.

- **Inclusion and belonging:** Using the correct name is an important element of fostering an inclusive and welcoming work environment. When people address you and your team by the correct name, it creates a sense of belonging and inclusivity. It signals that you are an integral part of the organization and that your contributions are valued.

- **Cultural sensitivity and diversity:** Correctly addressing individuals and teams by their preferred names is essential when working in diverse and multicultural environments. Respecting and honoring cultural naming conventions helps build trust, understanding, and positive relationships across different backgrounds.

- **Personal well-being:** Constantly hearing and being addressed by the wrong name may be emotionally distressing and impact your overall well-being. It may contribute to feelings of frustration, alienation, and even identity-related stress. Using the correct name promotes a healthier and more supportive work environment.

Using the correct names is more than a matter of accuracy; it is a reflection of your commitment to inclusivity and respect. When you address individuals and teams by their preferred names, you create an environment where everyone feels valued, recognized, and included. It reinforces your commitment to fostering a culture of respect and appreciation for diverse identities and experiences.

In our daily interactions, you often underestimate the power of using someone's correct name. It is a fundamental aspect of acknowledging and respecting their identity. I once experienced a situation where a customer consistently referred to me by different names, all starting with the same letter as my actual name. Eventually, she revealed that this was a deliberate negotiation strategy—a way to undermine my importance and gain an advantage in our business dealings.

Whether intentional or unintentional, not using the correct name or making only a partial effort to remember it can leave others feeling undervalued and unimportant. It sends a message that they are not significant enough for you to recognize and remember who they truly are. Remember, using someone's name is a simple yet powerful way to convey respect and make them feel seen and valued.

It's important to communicate the significance of using the correct name to those who repeatedly use the wrong one. Calmly and assertively reiterate the importance of your name and the impact it has on your well-being. If the issue persists and occurs in your place of work, consider involving higher management or human resources to address the situation.

As a business leader who intentionally rebrands teams for the good of the company, customers, and teammates' career development, I recognize the value of being relevant in a rapidly evolving business landscape, and the importance of career development for teammates. As this type of leader, I recognize and understand firsthand that rebranding teams and providing industry-standard job descriptions and career paths empower individuals, create growth opportunities, and foster a sense of purpose and fulfillment.

As examples, I have rebranded collections teams who focused on reactive payment demands from customers, putting stress on customer relationships, and proactive contract management teams who partner with customers to align on terms and conditions for ease of billing and payment processes, and if discrepancies occur, they resolve them by working with the customer in the short and long term, ultimately strengthening customer relationships. I have rebranded teams with company specific titles that unfortunately did not capture relevant industry standards and/or relatable career paths.

The intentional rebranding of these teams was effective on many levels throughout the organization and with customers, in managing the navigation of organizational dynamics, overcoming resistance to change, and ensuring a smooth transition aligning with industry standards. However, there continued to be a persistent issue where certain individuals continued to use the old team names, in meetings, presentations, and discussions. This type of inconsistency causes confusion and undermines the progress made in establishing clear services to customers, job descriptions, and career paths for the teams.

Yes, I have personally experienced the feelings that come along with frustration and feelings of being discounted. Dealing with longstanding challenges and biases is emotionally draining, especially when it affects your sense of recognition and self-worth. Here are a few suggestions to help you navigate this type of situation:

- **Recognize your value and expertise:** Remind yourself of your accomplishments, skills, and the value you bring to the organization. Focus on your professional achievements, the positive impact your team has made, and the recognition you've received from others who appreciate your work. By internalizing your own worth, you maintain confidence and resilience in the face of challenging situations.

- **Seek support from allies:** Identify colleagues, mentors, or leaders who are supportive and understanding. Share your concerns and experiences with them and seek their guidance and perspective. Allies provide emotional support, advice, and help amplify your voice within the organization. Lean on these supportive relationships for encouragement and affirmation.

- **Build relationships and networks:** Invest in building relationships with other leaders, both within and outside your organization. Seek out opportunities for collaboration, mentorship, or networking with leaders who are open-minded and supportive. Expanding your network may help you gain broader exposure, develop new alliances, and counterbalance the negative experiences you've had with specific individuals.

- **Document instances and gather evidence:** Keep a record of instances where you feel discounted or marginalized, including specific dates, conversations, and any other relevant details. This documentation may be useful if you choose to escalate the issue or discuss it with higher management in the future. Having concrete evidence supports your case and helps to address the recurring problem.

- **Address the issue directly, if appropriate:** Depending on the relationship dynamics and your comfort level, consider addressing the issue directly with the individuals involved. Choose a time and place where you may have a calm and professional conversation. Express your concerns, share your feelings, and communicate the impact their actions have on you and your team. Approach the conversation with a goal of fostering understanding and seeking a resolution.

- **Engage higher management or human resources, if necessary:** If the issue persists despite your efforts, consider involving higher management or human resources. Share your experiences, concerns, and the steps you've taken to address the situation. Provide them with any evidence you have documented. Higher management or human resources may provide guidance, support, and potentially initiate actions to address the underlying bias and create a more inclusive work environment.

Remember, you have the right to be addressed by your correct name, and advocating for this respect is crucial for creating an inclusive and respectful workplace.

## 34. Believe What You Would Love Is Already Yours

In the depths of our hearts, we all hold desires that feel out of reach; dreams that whisper to us in quiet moments, urging us to embrace them. Yet, too often, we find ourselves trapped in the belief that these aspirations are unattainable, locked away in a realm of wishful thinking. We yearn for something more, and yet doubt, uncertainty, and fear hold us back.

Let's consider the word "excited" and its subtle influence on your mindset. While it is often associated with enthusiasm and anticipation, it inadvertently evokes feelings of undeserving or skepticism. For instance, when someone says, "I'm so excited about this new job, it almost feels too good to be true," the word "excited" carries a sense of skepticism or disbelief. To overcome this, replace "excited" with "enthusiastic" or "passionate." By saying, "I'm passionate about this new job and ready to embrace the opportunities it brings," you create a positive and deserving mindset that allows you to fully embrace and appreciate the experience without any reservations.

What if I told you that the key to unlocking your deepest desires lies within you? What if I shared with you a powerful shift in perspective that may transform your relationship with your dreams? It begins by understanding that what you want may evolve into what you would love, and ultimately, what is already yours.

**The Power of "I Would Love":** As a life coach, I have witnessed firsthand the incredible transformation that occurs when my clients shift their language and mindset from "I want" to "I would love." It may seem like a simple shift in words, and yet its impact is profound. When you start expressing your desires with the phrase "I would love," something remarkable happens—you connect with the essence of what truly lights you up, what aligns with your authentic self.

Imagine the shift from longing and lack to a sense of anticipation and certainty. For example, the transition from "I want a fulfilling career," to "I would love a career that ignites my passion and allows me to make a meaningful impact." Do you feel the difference? By using the language of love, you infuse your desires with intention, clarity, and a deep knowing that what you yearn for is possible and already within your grasp.

**Discovering What You Would Love:** Embarking on the journey from "I want," to "I would love," requires a willingness to explore and discover the true desires that reside within you. It involves peeling back the layers of societal expectations, limiting beliefs, and self-imposed barriers to reveal the essence of your authentic dreams.

As your trusted guide and life coach, my role is to create a safe and empowering space where you may delve into the depths of your heart's desires. Together, we uncover the passions that stir your soul, the experiences that fill you with joy, and the goals that resonate with your true self. Through powerful questioning, self-reflection, and transformative exercises, we navigate the path from uncertainty to clarity, from doubt to unwavering belief.

**Embracing the Feeling of Ownership:** Once you have identified what you would love, we work together to cultivate the feeling of ownership—the unshakable belief that your desires are already yours. This is a pivotal moment, where the energy of creation begins to flow effortlessly towards you. You experience a shift in your confidence, in your actions, and in the way you show up in the world.

Put one foot in front of the other and watch as your confidence grows with each stride. Embody the feeling of living the life you would love—a life filled with purpose, abundance, and joy. Rewrite your story, replacing doubts and fears with unwavering faith in your abilities.

**Putting One Foot in Front of the Other:** Remember, this journey is not about instant transformation or overnight success. It is about taking consistent steps forward, no matter how small they may seem. Each positive word, each conscious thought, and each aligned action is a step closer to the life you would love.

Celebrate the progress you make along the way and be gentle with yourself when challenges arise. Trust that the universe is conspiring in your favor, and with each step, you are aligning yourself with the limitless possibilities that await.

**FINO (Feel Invited Not Obligated) Invitation:** I invite you to take a moment and reflect on what you want today that feels out of reach. Consider the possibility that what you yearn for evolves into what you would love—something that is already yours. Imagine the joy, fulfillment, and empowerment that come with living a life aligned with your deepest desires.

The journey awaits you. It is time to claim the life you would love—a life where you do, be, have, give, and create in ways that fill your heart with joy and purpose. Together, let us embark on this empowering adventure, where the power of positive language guides us to a future filled with infinite possibilities.

If you are ready to embark on this transformative journey, to step into your true power and create a life you would love, I am here to continue to guide you every step of the way. Together, we dissolve the barriers of doubt and disbelief, unlocking your infinite potential and witnessing the magic that unfolds when you believe what you would love is already yours.

Are you ready to embrace your dreams and make them a reality? Your adventure awaits.

## 35. Become a Word Minimalist to Shift Results

In your journey to harness the power of words, it is essential to become a word minimalist. By consciously removing disempowering words from your vocabulary, you elevate the impact of your sentences and communicate with clarity and confidence.

As you engage in this process of word minimization, be mindful that the removal of the words "can' and/or "try" is a powerful move. While they may be useful in certain contexts, they are often unnecessary and subtly undermine your message. By eliminating "can" and "try," you reinforce your abilities and convey a sense of determination. For example, consider the difference between "I can try to lose weight" or "I am trying to lose weight," compared to "I am committed to losing weight" or "I am losing weight." The latter statements demonstrate a commitment to your choice of action and leave no room for doubt.

Another word to minimize is "will." While it may seem innocuous, "will" often creates a sense of distance between you and your desired outcome. By removing "will," you bring the experience closer, as if it is already within your grasp. For instance, compare "I will achieve my goals," with "I achieve my goals"; or "How you will define success matters," with "How you define success matters." The latter statements instill a sense of confidence and certainty, reinforcing your capabilities.

In the spirit of empowering your language, it's important to recognize words that hold you back rather than propel you forward. One such word is "also." While seemingly harmless, "also" often sneaks into your sentences without adding any significant value. By intentionally removing "also" from your vocabulary, you create space for stronger, more impactful expressions. Let us embrace the power of clarity and purpose in your words, allowing them to shine brightly and make a meaningful difference in your life and the lives of those around you.

Here's an example of a sentence that demonstrates the removal of the word "also":

- Original sentence: "I love to dance, and I also enjoy painting."

- Revised sentence: "I love to dance, and I enjoy painting."

By eliminating the word "also," the revised sentence maintains the same meaning while presenting a more concise and direct expression. This allows the focus to remain on the activities being mentioned without the unnecessary addition of "also."

Remember, every word you choose has the power to shape your reality and the way others perceive you. By becoming a word minimalist, you strip away the unnecessary and allow the strength of your intentions and messages to shine through. Take a moment to review your writing and speech, identify disempowering words, and replace them with choices that amplify your voice and empower your communication.

By adopting the practice of word minimization, you align your language with your intentions and create a powerful impact on yourself and those around you.

## 36. Celebrate Success

In your journey of personal growth and self-improvement, it is important to invest the time to celebrate your successes, including the progress you make along the journey. By acknowledging and honoring your achievements, you cultivate a positive mindset and reinforce the belief in your ability to create positive change.

One subtle word that often goes unnoticed and has the power to undermine your celebration is "some." This seemingly harmless word diminishes the impact of your progress and minimizes the results you have achieved. Consider the following examples:

"I made some progress on my project," vs. "I made progress on my project." By removing "some" from the sentence, you shift the focus from minimal progress to the act of making progress itself. This change empowers you to recognize and appreciate the steps you have taken—your progress.

"I have some accomplishments to be proud of," vs. "I have accomplishments to be proud of."

Removing "some" from this sentence allows you to fully embrace your accomplishments and feel a genuine sense of pride. It acknowledges that you have achieved meaningful results and encourages you to celebrate them without reservation.

"I received some positive feedback from my colleagues," vs. "I received positive feedback from my colleagues."

By eliminating "some" from the sentence, you elevate the significance of the positive feedback you received. It reinforces the value of the recognition and encourages you to embrace and appreciate the support and encouragement you have received.

These examples demonstrate how the word "some" subtly downplays achievements and hinders the ability to fully celebrate success. By removing it, you open yourself up to a greater sense of empowerment and happiness. Embrace the progress you have made and the results you have achieved. Celebrate your success wholeheartedly and allow yourself to bask in the joy and fulfillment that come with acknowledging your accomplishments.

The influence of "some" and its impact on our mindset extends beyond ourselves; it applies to how we communicate with others. In the same way the word "some" undermines your own progress and achievements, using it when referring to others diminishes their accomplishments as well. By recognizing this and consciously eliminating disempowering words like "some," you create space for celebration and cultivate a positive mindset that propels you forward, empowering you and others to fully celebrate and appreciate the progress made, fostering a positive and supportive environment of growth and success.

# CHAPTER SEVEN

## What If ...

*"Shoot for the moon.*
*Even if you miss, you'll land among the stars."*
**– Les Brown**

## 37. Negative Words Are Wasted Energy

Words are more than a means of communication; they carry immense power and energy. Every word you utter has the potential to shape your reality, impact your experiences, and influence the way you perceive the world. It is through your words that you express your desires, beliefs, and intentions. Have you ever considered that the language you use, especially the negative words you employ, hinders your progress and keeps you stuck?

Words are energy in motion, vibrating through the universe and shaping the fabric of your existence. They act as a magnet, attracting similar energies and experiences into your life. When you consistently use negative words, you unknowingly focus your energy on what you don't want, inadvertently inviting more of it into your reality.

One peculiar aspect of language is that the universe does not hear the word "not." It doesn't recognize the negation in your statements. So, when you say, "I do not want to be stressed," the universe registers it as "I want to be stressed." By placing your attention and energy on what you do not want, you unintentionally reinforce the very experiences you wish to avoid.

To break free from this cycle and harness the true power of language, consciously shift your focus and energy from what you don't want, to what you would love. It is through positive and intentional language that you align yourself with your desires and manifest the experiences you truly seek.

**How to Identify Negative Words:**

Recognizing and reframing negative words in your vocabulary is an essential step towards transformation. Here are some common examples of negative words and phrases to be mindful of:

- **"Can't" and "impossible":** These words limit your potential and create a sense of powerlessness. Instead, replace them with empowering statements such as "I can" or "I am capable of."

- **"Failure" and "mistake":** These words carry a heavy burden of judgment and self-criticism. Shift your perspective by viewing them as opportunities for growth, learning, and improvement.

- **"Problem" and "obstacle":** These words emphasize challenges and create a negative mindset. Reframe them as "challenges" or "opportunities," highlighting the potential for growth and creative problem-solving.

- **"Never" and "always":** These words imply permanence and limit our belief in change. Replace them with words like "in certain situations" or "up until now," allowing for flexibility and the shift to the possibility of positive outcomes.

- **"Hate" and "dislike":** These words carry strong negative emotions and drain our energy. Practice expressing your preferences with neutral or positive language, focusing on what you enjoy or appreciate.

By consciously choosing positive and empowering words, you direct your energy towards what you would love to experience. Instead of saying, "I don't want to be alone," shift your focus to, "I would love to cultivate fulfilling relationships." Notice the difference in how these statements make you feel and the energy they radiate.

You may notice certain words reinforce your feelings. For example, if you feel tired, and you say "I am so tired," notice how you may begin to feel even more tired and often yawn as you speak the words.

I encourage you to pay close attention to the language you use in your daily life. Consider the impact of your words on your thoughts, emotions, and experiences. Shift your focus from the negative to the positive, from what you don't want, to what you would love. By consciously choosing uplifting and empowering language, you align yourself with the abundant possibilities that await you.

Let your words be a reflection of your desires, a catalyst for positive change, and a magnet for the experiences you long to manifest. Embrace the power of positive language and watch as your life transforms with newfound confidence and alignment with your deepest desires.

## 38. Replace Negative Words with Positive Ones

Changing your language from negative to positive is a powerful practice to transform your thoughts, emotions, and experiences. By consciously replacing negative words with positive ones, you shift your energy and mindset towards a more empowering and uplifting perspective. In this section, I guide you on how to quickly make this change in the moment when you encounter negative words or phrases, both in spoken and written communication.

**Awareness and Mindfulness:** The first step in replacing negative words with positive ones is to cultivate awareness and mindfulness of the language you use. Pay close attention to your thoughts, conversations, and written communication. Notice when negative words or phrases arise and become aware of their impact on your emotions and mindset.

**Restating Sentences Out Loud:** When you catch yourself using negative words or phrases in your spoken communication, take a moment to restate your sentence using positive language. For example, if you find yourself saying, "I can't do this," quickly rephrase it as, "I am capable of finding a solution to do this." By consciously deciding to create this shift, you redirect your focus towards possibilities and open yourself up to positive outcomes.

**Rewriting Texts and Emails:** In written communication, such as texts or emails, it's equally important to replace negative words or phrases with positive alternatives. When you come across negative language in your message, pause for a moment and rewrite it on the spot. Instead of writing, "I don't have time for this," reframe it as, "I choose to invest my time in other things today and schedule another time to prioritize this." By reframing your words, you convey a more positive message and reinforce a positive mindset within yourself.

**Immediate Replacement:** The key to effectively replacing negative words with positive ones is to make the change immediately in the moment of awareness. Avoid procrastination or leaving it for later. The more swiftly you replace the negative language, the more impact it has on your mindset and overall outlook.

**Practice and Repetition:** Like any new habit, replacing negative words with positive ones requires practice and repetition. Be patient with yourself as you navigate this transformation. The more you engage in this practice, the more natural and effortless it becomes. Over time, begin to notice a shift in your thought patterns and the language you naturally use, leading to a more positive and empowering perspective.

By actively replacing negative words with positive ones, both in spoken and written communication, you reclaim your power over your thoughts and experiences. This practice uplifts your own mindset and influences how others perceive you and the energy you bring to your interactions. Remember, every word holds energy, and by consciously choosing positive language, you align yourself with the abundance and possibilities that surround you.

Embrace the opportunity to transform your language, and watch as your inner dialogue and external experiences align with your desires and aspirations. Make it a habit to replace negative words with positive ones and witness the profound impact it has on your overall well-being and the manifestation of your dreams.

## 39. The Story You Tell Yourself Is the One That Comes True

Have you ever stopped to consider the impact of the words you tell yourself? Every thought, every affirmation, and every story you internalize has the power to shape your reality. The words you choose become the lens through which you perceive the world and determine the outcomes you experience. In this section, we explore the profound influence of self-talk and discover practical tips to transform your results by changing your story.

**The Language of Creation:** Words hold tremendous power. They are the outward expression of your thoughts and beliefs, and they shape your perception of yourself and the world around you. When you tell yourself negative or limiting thoughts, you reinforce and strengthen the barriers that hold you back from what is possible. Conversely, when you choose positive and empowering words, you create a pathway for growth, abundance, and success.

**Remember to Understand the Power of Thoughts and Feelings:** Your thoughts and feelings are intimately interconnected. The thoughts you cultivate generate emotions, which in turn influence your actions and shape your results. It is crucial to recognize that your thoughts are not fixed; they may be consciously chosen and directed. By aligning your self-talk with positive and empowering thoughts, you transform your emotional state and open yourself up to a world of possibilities.

**Tips for Changing Your Story**

**Awareness:** Begin by becoming aware of the words and narratives you habitually tell yourself. Notice the negative self-talk, the limiting beliefs, and the words that reinforce a sense of lack or impossibility. Awareness is the first step towards transformation.

**Positive Reframing:** Once you identify negative self-talk, reframe it into positive statements. Replace phrases like "I can't," with "I have chosen," and "I'm not good enough," with "I am more than enough." By consciously reframing your self-talk, you shift your focus from limitations, to empowerment of choice and possibilities.

**Empowering Affirmations:** Create a list of affirmations that reflect the reality you would love to experience. Affirmations are positive statements that affirm your desired outcomes and reinforce empowering beliefs. Repeat these affirmations daily and let them become the foundation of your self-talk.

**Surround Yourself with Positivity:** Pay attention to the people you surround yourself with and the media you consume. Surround yourself with individuals who uplift and inspire you, and engage in activities that promote positivity and personal growth. This supports you in maintaining a positive mindset and reinforcing empowering self-talk.

**Practice Self-Compassion:** Changing your self-talk takes time and effort. Be patient with yourself and practice self-compassion throughout the journey. Celebrate wins and acknowledge the progress you are making. Remember that every positive word you choose brings you closer to creating the reality you desire.

The words you tell yourself have a profound influence on your reality. By choosing positive and empowering self-talk, you may rewrite your story and manifest the outcomes you desire. Take ownership of your words, embrace the power they hold, and let them shape a future filled with abundance, success, and joy. Believe in the transformative power of your self-talk and watch as your life unfolds in alignment with the words you choose to embrace.

# 40. The Words You Choose Have the Power to Help Others

Words possess an incredible capacity to impact your own life and the lives of those around you. The words you choose have the potential to inspire, uplift, and empower others. In this section, we explore the profound influence of your words on the well-being and growth of the people in your life. By consciously selecting words that promote understanding, kindness, and encouragement, you become a catalyst for positive change and help others on their own transformative journeys.

**The Ripple Effect of Your Words:** Every word you speak has the power to create a ripple effect in the lives of those who hear them. Your words may uplift spirits, provide solace, and instill confidence. They have the ability to heal wounds, ignite passion, and inspire action. By choosing your words intentionally, you cultivate an environment of support, love, and growth.

**Lead by Example:** Often, the most effective way to help others is by embodying the qualities and principles you wish to instill in them. Your words serve as a beacon, guiding others towards a path of positivity and growth. When you choose words that reflect empathy, understanding, and respect, you become a source of inspiration and a role model for others to emulate.

**Conscious Communication:** Conscious communication begins with self-awareness. Take a moment to reflect on the impact of your words before they leave your lips. Ask yourself, "Do these words bring value to the lives of others? Do they inspire and uplift?" By consciously choosing your words, you create a space for open dialogue, understanding, and connection.

**The Power of Encouragement:** One of the most significant ways you help others through your words is by offering genuine encouragement. Celebrate their achievements, acknowledge their efforts, and provide words of support during challenging times. Your words provide the motivation and belief for someone to overcome obstacles and realize their full potential.

**Creating an Empowering Environment:** Consider the environment you wish to foster in your interactions with others. Let your words be a catalyst for positive change. Speak words of affirmation, gratitude, and encouragement. Use your words to create a safe and nurturing space where others feel seen, heard, and valued. Embrace the power of active listening, empathy, and compassion in your conversations.

**Inspiring Others to Be Their Best:** Your words have the potential to awaken the dormant greatness within others. Use them to ignite passion, stir creativity, and encourage personal growth. Offer constructive feedback with kindness and sincerity, and share insights that help others expand their perspectives. With your words, you inspire others to embrace their true potential and live a life filled with purpose and fulfillment.

As an example, notice the profound impact of your response when someone opens up and shares something vulnerable with you. Have you ever observed that when you respond with a simple "I'm sorry," the person often becomes emotional or even starts to cry? The reason behind this is that by saying "I'm sorry," you inadvertently place the burden on them, leaving them uncertain about how to respond. They might feel obligated to comfort you or downplay their own emotions. Instead, try a different approach. Respond with genuine gratitude by saying, "Thank you for sharing that with me. You should be so proud of your strength and courage." Then offer your support by asking, "Is there anything I could do to help you?" Notice the comfort and empowerment that emerges from this communication. Reflect on the profound difference your words make in providing a safe space for others to express themselves authentically and seek the support they truly need.

This type of response acknowledges the person's vulnerability, celebrates their strength, and offers practical support. It encourages a deeper connection and shows that you are present and genuinely care. By adopting this approach, you create an environment where people feel comfortable sharing their experiences and seeking assistance, fostering a culture of compassion, understanding, and genuine support.

In summary, as you see, the words you choose hold immense power. They have the ability to shape the world around you and make a profound impact on the lives of others. By consciously selecting words that uplift, inspire, and encourage, you become an agent of positive change. Embrace the responsibility that comes with your words and use them to create a supportive and empowering environment. Through the transformative power of your words, you help others discover their own inner strength, unleash their potential, and embark on a journey of growth and fulfillment.

## 41. There Is a New Universal Language

Imagine a world where your words become the building blocks of a new universal language; a language that transcends boundaries, unifies hearts, and ignites positive change. This book holds within its pages the potential to usher in such a transformative shift. It invites you to embrace the consistent use of positive words as the key that unlocks a new way of communication, one that empowers all of us to create the desired results we seek.

In the journey towards this new universal language, you are called to release the limiting contractions you have learned in school. These contractions, often containing "not" or negative expressions, no longer serve your highest aspirations. Instead, shift your focus towards positive words and empower yourself to speak of what you would love to do, and envision a world free from self-imposed limitations.

As you commit to maintaining a consistent flow of positive language, you begin to witness the birth of a new collective consciousness. Each individual's effort adds to the collective energy, amplifying the impact of positive words spoken by everyone. It is a conscious choice to break free from the old patterns and embrace a language that aligns our thoughts, feelings, actions, and results towards a shared vision of a better world.

While crafting this book, I, as the author, have been mindful of the language used to describe situations, understanding the importance of avoiding appropriation or misuses of words. Though I may stumble at times, my intention remains focused on fostering a language of positivity, empowerment, and unity.

By adopting this new universal language, you tap into the immense power that lies within each word you choose. You create a ripple effect that transcends individual lives, permeating communities, and ultimately, transforming the world. Together, we have the capacity to shape a reality where positive words become the norm, where conversations are infused with compassion, encouragement, and possibility.

As you embark on this journey with me, let us recognize the incredible potential within us to bring about lasting change through the consistent use of positive words. Embrace this new universal language, and let it be the thread that weaves our thoughts, feelings, actions, and results into a tapestry of unity, growth, and collective empowerment.

Together, we have the power to create a world where our words truly reflect our highest aspirations and support the realization of our deepest desires. Let us embark on this transformative endeavor, rewriting the narrative of our lives and shaping a future that is defined by love, possibility, and unlimited potential.

## 42. What if It Were Easy?

Within each of us lies a unique set of skills and abilities, waiting to be harnessed and utilized to their fullest potential. As a guide on your journey, I possess a keen eye for patterns, a talent for deciphering hidden codes that shape our experiences. One such code exists within the words you use and encounter every day—a secret language that reveals the depths of your confidence or the lack thereof. By unraveling this code, lies the key to unlock opportunities to grow in confidence and transform your experiences into ones driven by vision and joy.

Take a moment to reflect on the patterns in the words that surround you—the conversations you have, the media you consume, and the thoughts that fill your mind. Notice how often negativity seeps into the fabric of your language, weaving doubt, fear, and limitation into your everyday expression. These patterns may have become so ingrained that they go unnoticed, subtly undermining your confidence and shaping the lens through which you perceive the world.

What if I told you that you have the power to shift these patterns effortlessly? By increasing your awareness and choosing to change the words you use, you embark on a transformative journey. It begins with recognizing the patterns that no longer serve you and replacing them with empowering and positive expressions.

The beauty of this process lies in its ease. Once you develop an acute awareness of the words you choose, you begin to notice the patterns with greater clarity. It becomes effortless to identify the language that disempowers you, and equally effortless to choose words that uplift, inspire, and create positive change. By changing your outward expression through the conscious selection of words, you naturally and easily change your inward expression of yourself.

Imagine the impact this simple shift could have on your confidence, your relationships, and your experiences. By infusing your language with positivity, by intentionally choosing words that reflect your vision and values, you reshape your reality. You create a vibrant tapestry of joy, abundance, and possibility that unfolds effortlessly before you.

I invite you to embrace the power of easy transformation. Become an observer of the patterns within your language and the world around you. Notice how negativity sneaks in and begins to erode your confidence. And then, with a newfound awareness, make the conscious choice to change those patterns, one word at a time.

As you embark on this journey of word mastery, you may begin to witness the remarkable transformation that unfolds within you. The subtle shift in your language creates a ripple effect, elevating your confidence, amplifying your joy, and magnetizing positive experiences into your life. Embrace the ease with which you transform your reality and open yourself to a world where it truly is easy to grow in confidence and manifest your deepest desires.

Are you ready to unlock the power of easy transformation through the words you choose? Join me on this journey, and together, let us create a tapestry of uplifting language, empowering patterns, and a life filled with limitless possibilities.

# CHAPTER EIGHT

## Rise Up

*"With the new day comes new strength."*
**– Eleanor Roosevelt**

## 43. Retire Sizes

One aspect we haven't delved into yet is the impact of sizes in our language. The words you choose to describe your goals, dreams, and achievements hold tremendous power over your thoughts and feelings. Consider the word "big." When you label something as big, you unconsciously make it larger than yourself, elevating it to a level that seems beyond your reach. Conversely, words like "small" diminish the value and significance of what you are discussing. These common words shape your perception and either empower or limit you.

Take a moment to reflect on how frequently you hear and use phrases like "that's too big of an effort" or "it's just a small thing." These statements may seem harmless, and yet they subtly influence your mindset and actions. By making something bigger or smaller than yourself, you relinquish your own power and believe that the struggle is greater than your capabilities. You unwittingly assign authority to the size of the issue and hinder your own potential.

Consider the effect these words have on you personally and those around you. How does it feel when you describe your goals or achievements as big or small? Notice how minimizing or exaggerating the effort diminishes the value you add and undermines your confidence. When you use words like "big" or "large," you unintentionally magnify the challenges and make them appear insurmountable. Conversely, describing something as "small" or "little" downplays the significance of accomplishments.

Let's explore an alternative approach. What if you replaced these size-focused words with more positive and empowering language? Instead of saying, "I took a big step," you could say, "I took a significant step forward." By reframing your words, you align your perception with the reality of the situation. Recognize that every action, regardless of its perceived size, contributes to growth and progress. It's not about making it seem like a giant leap when it was merely a small step; it's about acknowledging the value of each individual step taken on the journey.

I invite you to retire the sizes and retire the limitations they impose. Remove words like big, small, little, large, and a lot, from your vocabulary when describing your efforts and achievements and those of others. Instead, embrace the step for what it is—an essential part of progress. Celebrate each milestone, recognizing the impact it has on personal growth, and the positive ripple effect it creates in your life and the lives of others.

As you become more aware of the words you use and the patterns they create, you witness a shift in perception and self-belief. By choosing words that accurately reflect the true value and impact of actions, you empower yourself and others to reach new heights. Every step, no matter its size, matters. Embrace the power of language, retire the sizes, and celebrate the journey every step of the way.

Do you feel the liberation that comes with letting go of these limiting words? Do you imagine the transformation that occurs when you choose words that uplift and empower? Together, let's create a world where our language supports our desired results, where positive words consistently flow and connect us in a universal language of possibility, growth, and joy.

## 44. Remove Static & Confusion

To truly master the art of clear communication and remove static and confusion completely from our words, you must delve deeper into the process of eliminating unnecessary noise and interference. Let's explore some effective strategies and techniques to help you achieve this goal.

**Mindfulness and Intention:** Cultivating mindfulness and intention in your communication is key to removing static. Before speaking, take a moment to ground yourself and become fully present. Set a clear intention for your communication: What do you want to convey? How do you want the listener to feel or respond? By bringing focused awareness to your words, you may eliminate distractions and deliver a more impactful message.

**Active Listening and Feedback:** Actively listening to others and seeking feedback may provide valuable insights into areas where static may still persist in your communication. Engage in active listening by giving your full attention to the speaker, observing their non-verbal cues, and asking clarifying questions when needed. Actively seek feedback from trusted individuals who may help pinpoint any lingering static in your speech patterns.

**Eliminating Filler Words:** Building upon what was discussed earlier, continue to practice eliminating filler words from your speech. Be patient with yourself, as breaking habits takes time and consistent effort. Increase your self-awareness during conversations, presentations, or even casual interactions. Whenever you catch yourself using a filler word, pause, take a breath, and rephrase your statement with clarity and purpose.

**Powerful Non-Verbal Communication:** Remember that communication is not solely reliant on words. Non-verbal cues, such as body language, facial expressions, and tone of voice, play a significant role in conveying your message. Pay attention to your non-verbal communication, ensuring that it aligns with the clarity and intention of your words. Practice open and confident body language, maintain eye contact, and speak with conviction to enhance your overall communication effectiveness.

**Preparation and Structure:** Effective communication often benefits from adequate preparation and structure. When entering important conversations or presentations, take the time to organize your thoughts and outline key points. Having a clear structure in mind may help you be on track and deliver your message with greater precision. Practice delivering your message in a concise and coherent manner, focusing on clarity and eliminating unnecessary details or tangents.

**Seek Professional Development:** Consider investing in professional development opportunities that specifically focus on improving communication skills. Attend workshops, seminars, or courses that provide guidance on effective communication techniques, public speaking, or persuasive language. Engaging in structured learning may equip you with tools and strategies to remove static and enhance your overall communication abilities.

**Practice, Practice, Practice:** Finally, the key to removing static completely lies in consistent practice. Incorporate intentional communication exercises into your daily routine. Engage in role-playing scenarios, record and review your own speeches or presentations, or seek opportunities to engage in public speaking or group discussions. The more you practice, the more confident and comfortable you become in delivering clear and compelling messages.

By incorporating these strategies and embracing the mindset of continuous improvement, you gradually remove static from your communication, allowing your words to resonate authentically and powerfully with others. Remember, effective communication is a lifelong journey, and each step you take towards eliminating static brings you closer to becoming a master communicator.

In the following chapters, we explore advanced techniques, case studies, and practical exercises to further enhance your communication skills. Embrace the process, be committed, and witness the transformative impact of clear, intentional, and static-free communication in all areas of your life.

## 45. Know the Truth: Breaking Free from the Grip of Negative Words

Addiction to negative words is a silent thief that holds you back, keeping you stuck and eroding your self-confidence over time. It's a two-way path that reflects negative thoughts and, in turn, reinforces them, leading to a cascade of negative emotions, actions, or even the lack thereof. These patterns ultimately diminish the chances of experiencing true joy and success in results. There is a way out, a path to liberation and transformation.

Imagine treating this addiction to negative words as you would approach recovery from any other addiction. Create a support group, offer forgiveness to yourself, and embark on a journey of personal growth. In these steps, you embark on our own version of recovery, replacing negative words with positive ones and building the courage and confidence to pursue your deepest desires.

You may have come across advice on avoiding negative self-talk and loving yourself, which are undeniably valuable practices. However, what sets the approaches herein apart is the focus on patterns of words—addictions to ways of communication, and insights to a code of words for recovery habits to take you on a transformational journey in addressing the profound connection between the words you choose and your thoughts, unveiling the transformative power they hold over your life.

Here lies the truth: The key to transformation in any area of your life lies in discovering what you truly desire, and mustering the courage to implement the necessary changes. And at the core of this transformation is the power of your words.

Learn how to wield this power, to break free from the clutches of repeated patterns and addiction to negative words. It is through this liberation that you unlock the door to a brighter future. You have the capacity to transform any area of your life, and as the first step, confront and overcome addiction to negative words.

Negative words manifest in various ways, including negative self-talk, put-downs, hesitation, procrastination, rumination, discouragement, lack of courage, lack of confidence, and fear. These words weave themselves into the fabric of your thoughts, emotions, and actions, shaping your reality. Remember, addiction may be overcome, and negative words may be replaced.

As you continue on this transformative journey, you have the opportunity to discover the incredible power that lies within your words. By choosing positive and empowering language, you break free from the chains that have held you back. You cultivate a new way of being and communicating, one that propels you towards your dreams and allows you to embrace a life filled with joy, purpose, and success.

Are you ready to know the truth? Are you ready to reclaim your power and shape a future defined by your desires, rather than the constraints of negative words?

# 46. Begin to Transform Results

Beginning to transform your results requires a deliberate focus on the words you use. By incorporating positive and empowering language into every aspect of your life, you ignite a radiant energy within yourself and positively impact the lives of others. It is essential to eliminate the static and backward-pulling words that constrict and hold you back, replacing them with words that hold meaning and propel you towards a brighter future.

The truth of who you are, and the power of your words, go hand in hand. Every word you choose to speak reflects your inner essence. Take a moment to discern whether your words align with your authentic self. Are you speaking with humility or boldness? Are you expressing your deepest truth?

Let's examine a few examples where the intention may be to evoke a positive mindset, yet unintentionally the words chosen convey force and demand, which are misaligned with the intention to inspire and motivate.

| Disempowering Commands | Empowering, Uplifting Choice |
|---|---|
| Stay | Be |
| Hard | Easy |
| Make | Allow |

**Examples**
Stay Positive to Be Positive
Work Hard to Easy Work
Make it Happen to Allow it to Happen

As you embark on the journey of embracing your authentic self, remember that it is a continuous process. Although there may be times when you stray from your path, always know that you have the ability to course-correct.

Surround yourself with those who love and support you, drawing strength from their presence. Embrace the challenges and adversities you have faced, for they have molded you into the person you are destined to become.

In your pursuit of transforming your relationship with words, keep in mind that your truth remains steadfast. Hold unwaveringly to your authentic self, allowing its radiant light to illuminate your path. As you progress on this transformative journey, may you find solace, resilience, and a profound sense of purpose by being true to who you are. Let the power of positive words guide you towards increased joy and truly transformative experiences.

# CHAPTER NINE

## Shine Your Light

*"The effect you have on others*
*is the most valuable currency there is."*
*– Jim Carrey*

## 47. Turn up the Volume Every Day

In today's world, the power to change lies within the conscious choice to shine your light through your words each day. It may seem like a simple task, and yet it holds great significance. Those who understand how to turn up the volume on their words share the true power within themselves and positively impact the world through their interactions.

Let's delve into a few examples that demonstrate the transformative impact of word substitutions. Consider the word "can," often used to express possibility. However, it implies uncertainty and leaves room for doubt. Furthermore, it may be interpreted as a directive that diminishes the feeling of choice, ultimately disempowering you. By replacing "can" with "I am" or "may," depending on the context, signifies that you have a choice, or using "to" to indicate an ongoing action, you claim ownership of your choices and empower yourself. Reflect on the difference between saying, "I can attract positive results" and "I am attracting positive results," or "Words help you feel empowered" versus "Words may help you feel empowered." In each example, the latter emphasizes the power within you, creating a stronger, more resolute intention, and allowing you to make a choice.

The decision to turn up the volume on your words and shine your light is a personal one. In her resiliency and unwavering love for her dreams, my daughter Marissa has shown me that each of us holds the power to turn up the light within ourselves and, consequently, spark a positive transformation in the world. It starts with recognizing that you have the ability to choose the language you use and the impact it has on others. By embracing the power of your words and consciously crafting them to uplift, inspire, and empower, you become a catalyst for change.

So, take a moment to reflect on the light within you. How do you intend to shine your light in the world? It all begins with the words you choose to express, connect, and create a positive ripple effect. Let your words be a symphony that resonates with joy, love, and transformation.

## 48. Take Inspired Action

Writing this book is an embodiment of inspired action for me. It is the means through which I express the contents of my heart and share the transformative power of words with the world. As you engage in this journey of self-discovery and immerse yourself in the pages of this book, I hope you feel a profound sense of confidence. By choosing to take inspired action, you are shining the light within yourself.

Let's explore the impact of word choices on taking action. Words like "must" and "have to" often carry a sense of obligation and force, leaving little room for personal choice and inspiration. By replacing these words with phrases like, "I choose to," "I would love to," or "I am," you reclaim your power to take action from a place of inspiration and desire. Consider the difference between saying, "I must complete this task" and "I choose to do this task with enthusiasm and passion." The latter statement reflects your personal agency and infuses the action with a sense of purpose and joy.

Taking inspired action is about aligning your choices with your deepest desires and passions. It is a conscious decision to move forward with intention, driven by the light that shines within you. As you immerse yourself in the teachings of this book and apply them to your life, may you feel empowered to take action in alignment with your authentic self.

Remember, every step you take on this journey of inspired action is a testament to your commitment to personal growth and transformation. By infusing your actions with intention, purpose, and love, you are shaping your own life and inspiring and uplifting those around you.

So, embrace the power of inspired action and allow it to propel you forward on your path. Take each step with intention, knowing that you have the ability to create a life filled with joy, fulfillment, and positive impact.

## 49. Harnessing the Power of Momentum

As you embark on the journey of transforming your language and shining the light within, it's important to recognize the significance of momentum. Momentum is the force that propels us forward, building upon our actions and choices, and creating a positive ripple effect in our lives and the lives of others. In this section, we explore how to cultivate and sustain momentum in our language transformation journey, and how to inspire and uplift others along the way.

**Embrace the Energy of Progress:** Every step you take towards conscious language usage and empowering word choices creates a momentum of its own. It's crucial to acknowledge and celebrate your progress, no matter how small. As you become more aware of the words you use and make intentional shifts, you are creating a positive shift in your mindset and your interactions. Embrace this energy of progress and let it fuel your determination to continue the journey.

**Cultivate a Growth Mindset:** A growth mindset is essential in maintaining momentum. Understand that transforming your language is an ongoing process, and it requires patience and perseverance. See challenges as opportunities for growth and learning. Instead of viewing setbacks as failures, embrace them as valuable lessons that propel you forward. By cultivating a growth mindset, you create fertile ground for momentum to thrive.

**Be Curious and Open:** As you gain momentum, it's important to remain curious and open-minded. Continually seek new knowledge, insights, and perspectives. Explore different resources, attend workshops, and engage in meaningful conversations. By expanding your understanding of language and its impact, you enhance your own transformation and gain the ability to inspire and guide others on their journeys.

**Share and Inspire:** One of the most powerful ways to sustain momentum is by sharing your experiences and inspiring others. As you witness the positive changes in your own life, extend a helping hand to those around you. Share your insights, stories, and strategies. Offer support and encouragement to others who are on their own language transformation paths. By uplifting and empowering others, you create a ripple effect of positive change that reverberates through communities and beyond.

**Leverage Momentum Science:** Momentum science tells us that small actions, when consistently applied, lead to significant transformations over time. Apply this principle to your language transformation journey. Commit to making small, incremental changes each day. Consistency is key. By consistently choosing empowering words and consciously shifting your language, you amplify the momentum and pave the way for greater growth and impact.

Momentum is a powerful force that drives us forward on our language transformation journey. Embrace the energy of progress, cultivate a growth mindset, be curious and open, and share your experiences to inspire others. By leveraging momentum science and taking small, consistent actions, you continue to gain momentum, creating a positive impact in your own life and in the lives of those around you. Keep moving forward, and let your momentum carry you towards a future filled with confidence, joy, and transformation.

## 50. Become Your Best Self

As you harness the momentum gained through your language transformation journey, you embark on a profound transformation—a journey of becoming your best self. This section is to delve into the profound impact of positive words, guiding you towards a life filled with authenticity, purpose, and fulfillment. By shedding the weight of negative words and embracing the power of positive language, you witness the emergence of your truest, most authentic self.

**Unleashing Your Authenticity:** As the layers of negative words fall away, a beautiful transformation takes place. You begin to express yourself with positive words in every interaction, conversation, and communication. With each word you choose, you become more aligned with your true essence. Day by day, you step into the person you were always meant to be—a reflection of your authentic self.

**Embracing Your Purpose:** Your language holds the key to unlocking your purpose. By consciously choosing positive words, you align your thoughts and actions with your deepest values and aspirations. As you gain clarity through your language transformation, you unveil your unique purpose and calling. Your words become a powerful instrument for manifesting your purpose and making a meaningful impact on the world around you.

**Empowering Others:** As you embody your best self, you become a beacon of inspiration and empowerment for others. Your positive language and authentic presence inspire those around you to embrace their own language transformations. By uplifting and supporting others on their journeys, you create a ripple effect of positive change that extends far beyond your individual sphere of influence.

**Transforming Every Aspect of Your Life:** The power of positive words transcends the boundaries of your profession or role. It permeates every facet of your existence. Whether it's in your personal relationships, professional endeavors, or everyday interactions, your newfound language empowerment accompanies you everywhere you go. It shapes your experiences, influences your decisions, and contributes to the creation of a life that aligns with your highest aspirations.

Through the momentum gained in your language transformation journey, you step into the radiant brilliance of your best self. By shedding the weight of negative words and embracing the transformative power of positive language, you unlock a profound sense of authenticity, purpose, and fulfillment. Your words become a reflection of your true essence, propelling you towards a life of joy, meaning, and impact.

Embrace this journey wholeheartedly, knowing that your words have the power to shape your reality and inspire others. As you become your best self, may your words illuminate your path, guide your actions, and create a legacy that resonates far beyond your own lifetime. Step into the fullness of who you were meant to be, and let your language be a testament to the limitless potential that resides within you.

# 51. Help Others

At the heart of this book lies a powerful intention: to help others. As you embark on your transformative journey of language empowerment, remember the profound impact you have on those around you. By using positive and empowering words, you become an agent of change, inspiring others to embrace their greatness and become the best versions of themselves. In the words of Jim Carrey, "The effect you have on others is the most valuable currency there is." Let us explore the art of uplifting and empowering others through the intentional use of language.

**The Power of Positive Words:** Your words possess immense power. By consciously choosing positive words, you create an environment that nurtures and uplifts others. Each interaction becomes an opportunity to empower, inspire, and encourage those you encounter. As you harness the power of your words, you become a catalyst for positive change in the lives of others.

**Creating a Ripple Effect:** Just as a pebble creates ripples that expand across a pond, your words have the potential to create a ripple effect in the lives of others. Through your language transformation, you elevate your own experience and ignite a spark within those who witness your transformation. By sharing your journey and supporting others on their paths, you create a powerful network of positive influence that amplifies the impact of your words.

**Inspiring Greatness:** As you embrace your best self and embody the power of positive language, you become a living example of what is possible. Your words inspire greatness in others, encouraging them to step into their own power and pursue their dreams. By lifting others up and helping them recognize their inherent worth, you play a vital role in shaping a world filled with empowered individuals.

**Spreading Kindness and Compassion:** Kindness and compassion are at the core of empowering others. By infusing your words with love, empathy, and understanding, you create a safe space for growth and transformation. Your words become a beacon of light, providing comfort and support to those who need it most. Through acts of kindness and the power of your positive language, you foster a culture of connection and unity.

As you continue on your journey of language empowerment, remember the profound effect you have on others. Your positive words and actions ignite a spark within them, inspiring them to embark on their own transformative journeys. By embracing the power of your language, you become a catalyst for positive change, creating a ripple effect that extends far beyond your immediate sphere of influence. Let the intention of this section guide you as you uplift and empower others, knowing that your impact is immeasurable and invaluable.

In the words of Jim Carrey, "The effect you have on others is the most valuable currency there is." Embrace this truth and let your words be a gift that enriches the lives of those around you. Together, let us create a world where positivity, empowerment, and transformation flourish, one word at a time.

# CHAPTER TEN

## Feel the Joy

*"Know what sparks the light in you.*
*Then use that light to illuminate the world."*
*– Oprah Winfrey*

# 10

## 52. Create New Goals to Grow in Joy

In the final chapter of this book, "Feel the Joy," we embark on a journey of personal transformation through the art of goal setting. Setting meaningful goals using the words "what," "why," "how," and "when" brings about breakthrough results and leads to a life filled with joy and fulfillment. In this section, I share with you a proven framework that I have used in my coaching business, business roles, and personal life to set goals and achieve success. Get ready to unlock your potential and create new goals that inspire and propel you forward.

### Designing Goals with the 4 Keys to Unlock Breakthrough Results

#### Key 1: What?
Start by identifying one thing you would love to do, be, have, or give. Ask yourself, "Would you love it?" Visualize yourself in that desired state, imagining what you would be doing, seeing, and hearing.

#### Key 2: Why?
Understand the deep-rooted reasons why this particular goal matters to you. Consider who else it impacts and why it holds significance. Make the connection between your personal values and the impact you know this goal has on you and others.

As you decide on the words you use to describe your "why," define your measure of success and ensure that your "why" is answered in this process. If your measure of success does not answer your "why," then continue to adjust your "why" and measure of success until they answer each other.

## Unlock Results

### Key 3: How?

Determine the actions you could take to begin working towards your goal. Explore various strategies and identify the most important actions to prioritize. Organize your plan by selecting, prioritizing, and scheduling the actions that resonate with you the most.

### Key 4: When?

Align your "what," "why," and "how" by defining how you measure success and setting a timeline for achieving your goal.

Measure your progress along the way and celebrate each milestone.

As an example:

**What:** Change careers.

**Why:** It matters because choosing a career that aligns with your passions and values is the key to unlocking a life of purpose, joy, and fulfillment. When you have the courage to pursue your true calling, you tap into your highest potential and unleash your unique gifts upon the world. Time and money freedom become the catalysts for this transformation, allowing you to break free from the constraints of a traditional job and embrace a path that brings you joy and meaning. By embracing this change, you create a ripple effect of inspiration, in your own life and in the lives of those you touch. It matters because when you have the freedom to live authentically and pursue your dreams, you become a living example of what is possible, igniting a flame of possibility in others. So, embrace the journey of career transformation and discover the profound impact it has on your life and the lives of those around you.

**How:** List options: Find a new job, start my own business, etc., and choose.

**When:** Find a new job in the next 6 months.

Remember, success lies in answering your "why," and not necessarily in completing every item on your action list. It's about the journey and the growth you experience along the way.

So, if you find a new job in 6 months, the question to measure success is:

Is your career aligned with your passions and values, unlocking a life of purpose, joy, and fulfillment? Do you have the courage to pursue your true calling and unleash your unique gifts upon the world? Are you experiencing time and money freedom that allows you to break free from the constraints of a traditional job and embrace a path that brings you joy and meaning? Are you creating a ripple effect of inspiration, igniting a flame of possibility in your own life and in the lives of those you touch? Are you living authentically and pursuing your dreams, becoming a living example of what is possible?

As you embark on your journey of career transformation, these questions serve as a measure of success in determining if your "why" is truly being answered. Reflect on these questions and assess whether your career choices align with the profound impact you desire for your life and the lives of those around you. Embrace the opportunities that arise, make courageous choices, and discover the transformative power of aligning your career with your passions and values.

If you did obtain a new job in 6 months, and the answer to any part of the "why" is NO, and your "why" was not fully answered, then success requires additional actions in the area of "how" and "when," until you do achieve success and/or choose to modify your "why," either in full because your "why" has changed, or in part because your "why" may involve multiple steps and you choose to measure the progress in multiple goals instead of one goal.

**BONUS:**

TAKE YOUR IDEAS FROM IMAGINATION TO A VISION WITH ACTIONS AND RESULTS YOU LOVE!

**CLAIM YOUR FREE BONUS,** 4 KEYS TO DESIGN YOUR GOALS & UNLOCK BREAKTHROUGH RESULTS, by visting www.WordsMatterToday.com and clicking on **"UNLOCK YOUR POTENTIAL,"** to DOWNLOAD YOUR FULL-SIZE, FULL-COLOR, PRINT-READY VERSION.

As you embrace this framework for goal setting, may you feel empowered to create new goals that align with your passions and values. Remember, the journey towards your goals is an opportunity for growth, joy, and transformation. Embrace each step with enthusiasm and let the process of setting and pursuing your goals fill your life with fulfillment and meaning.

## 53. Grow Confidence

Confidence is a powerful force that resides within your words. When you truly understand what lights you up, and you begin to share your talents with a feeling of joy, you then radiate that light to the world through your word choices, positive thoughts, feelings of joy, inspirational actions, and results. In this section, we explore the significance of eliminating the word "get" from your vocabulary as an example of a word that is considered a driver of stress and force, especially when working on your goals.

The word "get" implies a sense of lack, as if you do not have something and that there is question as to if you have the ability to attain it someday. However, that elusive "someday" never arrives. Let's take the example of saying, "I want to get an A on the test." This statement combines stress-inducing words like "want," with a sense of force in the word "get." It creates a feeling of distance and unattainability.

Instead, let's try a different approach. Say, "I would love to receive an A on the test." Notice the shift in your mindset. By using the phrase "would love to receive," you open your mind to the possibility of achieving what you desire. You choose to see the A on the test as something to receive. Do you feel the difference?

By consciously choosing empowering words, you cultivate a sense of confidence within yourself. You acknowledge that your goals and desires are within reach and that you have the power to attract and receive them. This simple shift in language has a profound impact on how you approach challenges and achieve your desired outcomes.

So, I invite you to pay attention to the words you use and the feelings they evoke. Choose words that uplift and empower you, replacing forceful or out-of-reach language with words that reflect possibility and choice. Embrace the confidence that comes from knowing that your desires are within your grasp, waiting for you to receive them.

How does it feel to create a shift in your words? Do you sense the growing confidence within you as you choose language that supports your dreams and aspirations? Embrace the power of your words and watch as your confidence blossoms, leading you to greater heights of success and fulfillment.

## 54. Transform Life Experiences Today

Life is a precious gift, and none of us know how much time we have on this Earth. It is a reminder that every moment is valuable and should be cherished. In this section, I encourage you to embrace the transformative power of positive words and take action today.

Life is short, and it's important to make the most of the experiences you have. Positive words have the remarkable ability to connect people and create a sense of support and understanding. They have the power to uplift, inspire, and brighten the lives of those around us. When you choose your words consciously, you contribute to a positive and uplifting environment that enriches your own experiences as well as those of others.

In a world that may sometimes feel divided and disconnected, the impact of positive words becomes even more significant. They have the power to bridge gaps, foster empathy, and bring people closer together. By choosing words that uplift, encourage, and show kindness, you contribute to a collective energy of support and love.

In life, there are moments that challenge us to our core, pushing us to redefine who we are and how we navigate the world. For me, one of those defining moments was when I received a breast cancer diagnosis. The words we use in such circumstances hold tremendous power, shaping our perception and response to the challenges we face.

Initially, I found myself saying, "I have cancer," and my husband, Jay, my pillar of strength, gently corrected me. He reminded me that this was an event—a temporary chapter in our lives—and that we would face it together with unwavering determination. His words of support and perspective made all the difference, empowering me to confront the situation head-on.

Yet, there were moments when I felt a profound shift within myself. It was as if my identity was altered, and the person I once knew no longer existed. I struggled to convince myself that I was still the same, and the truth was, I had been forever changed from the moment I heard the diagnosis.

The key, was for me to focus on finding the good in the situation and begin to re-write the story on what I could gain from this experience.

I began by acknowledging that my awareness had deepened. I cultivated gratitude for the years of life and love I had been blessed with and envisioned the future I desired beyond the "cancer event." Though uncertain about what lies ahead, I embrace the fact that I have become a stronger, more resilient individual through this journey. Every day has become an opportunity to live fully and to cherish every moment, surrounded by the people and activities that bring me joy.

I share this personal story with you, knowing that it may resonate deeply within your own life's experiences. Whether you have faced a health diagnosis, witnessed a loved one's struggle, or endured the loss of someone dear, it is through our thoughts and words that we find solace and gratitude for the time we've had and the newfound possibilities before us.

Moreover, a shift in your words and thoughts applies to health diagnoses and to any form of loss you may encounter in life. Whether it's a relationship breakup, the passing of a loved one, the arrival of a new life, or the battle against addiction, the power of gratitude remains steadfast. By reflecting on what once was with a grateful heart, you honor the memories, the lessons, and the growth that came from those experiences. You embrace the notion that every ending carries within it the seeds of new beginnings. From the ashes of what was, we imagine the beauty of what may be—the transformative potential that lies in front of you. It is through this lens of gratitude and possibility that you navigate life's challenges with resilience, grace, and an unwavering belief in the limitless possibilities that await us.

Remember, the power of positive language and intentional thoughts shape our perception and response to life's challenges. May this chapter in your journey be an inspiration to choose words that uplift, empower, and affirm your resilience. Embrace the strength within you, for you are capable of overcoming any obstacle and creating a future filled with love, purpose, and limitless possibilities.

So, I urge you to begin your transformation today. Embrace the understanding that life is short, and every moment is an opportunity for growth, connection, and joy. Choose positive words that inspire, encourage, and empower yourself and others. Embrace the beauty of human connection and the transformative power of language.

Let us create a world where positive words are the norm, where each interaction becomes an opportunity to uplift and support. Together, we transform our life experiences and make a positive impact on the lives of those around us. Start now, for today is a gift waiting to be embraced and transformed through the power of your words.

## 55. Create a Better Future for Generations to Come

In the section titled "Create a Better Future for Generations to Come," we delve into the profound impact our words have on shaping the world for future generations. As we reflect on the words of my daughter Jenna, who beautifully expressed the sentiment of being "the light of the future," I am reminded of the responsibility each of us carry, to leave a positive legacy for our children, grandchildren, and all those who follow.

I am grateful that my own family, with my husband, two daughters, and son, serves as a shining example of strength and authenticity. They have embraced doing what they love with their whole hearts, living as their true selves. Their commitment to growth, personal fulfillment, and making a difference is inspiring.

Through the insights and wisdom shared in this book, I hope to empower both you and your own family to continue on your journey of growth, self-discovery, and positive influence. By consciously choosing your words, embracing your authentic selves, and extending a helping hand to others, you may shape a better future for generations to come.

The impact of our words extends far beyond our immediate interactions. They have the power to ripple through time and influence the beliefs, actions, and choices of those who come after us. By being mindful of the words you use and the energy you bring into the world, you create a powerful and positive legacy that continues to resonate for generations.

Imagine a future where words are filled with love, compassion, and encouragement; a future where authenticity and empathy guide interactions, and where helping others becomes a natural expression of who we are, without fear of what others think, because it is positive and supportive.

As your children and grandchildren grow, may they continue to be beacons of light, illuminating the path for others to follow. May they use their words to uplift, inspire, and empower those around them. And may they pass on the wisdom they have gained to future generations, creating a world that is kinder, more compassionate, and filled with the transformative power of positive words.

Through your own journey and the insights shared in this book, may you and your family continue to evolve and positively influence the generations of the future. Together, let us create a legacy of love, authenticity, and empowerment that resonates for years to come.

## 56. Look Around

You are now invited to invest the time to pause and reflect on the transformative journey you have embarked on throughout this book. Take a moment to look around and absorb the lessons and insights you have encountered.

Imagine a world where everyone embraces the power of positive words. It would be a world where people feel seen, heard, and valued. It would be a world where differences are celebrated and compassion flows freely. By making a conscious choice to use positive words, you create a ripple effect that brightens your own life and the lives of those you encounter.

I am incredibly grateful for my amazing friend and hairdresser, Kady Landman. Kady is skilled in her profession and radiates positivity and genuine care for her clients. During one of our conversations, as I was discussing my book on the significance of words, Kady shared a profound insight that resonated deeply with me. She said, "If plants flourish when spoken to with kindness and positivity, imagine the incredible impact it could have on a person." Her words struck a chord within me, reminding me of the immense power we hold in our hands and the potential for growth and transformation that lies within each of us. Let us embrace this wisdom and recognize the incredible influence our words can have in nurturing and uplifting others, just like the nourishing words that help plants thrive.

Throughout this book, we have explored the transformative power of words, witnessing how they spark the light within us, shape our perceptions, and inspire positive change. We have delved into the importance of conscious language choices, understanding that the words we use shape our own reality and have the potential to uplift, encourage, and empower others.

Take a moment to reflect on your own journey through this book. Consider the shifts in awareness and perspective you have experienced. Notice how the conscious choice of words has impacted your interactions, your self-belief, and your ability to create positive change in your life and the lives of those around you.

As you look around, observe the people in your life—the ones you interact with daily, your loved ones, your colleagues, and even strangers. Imagine the transformative power of speaking positively to them, of using words that uplift, inspire, and affirm their inherent worth. Consider the ripple effect this may have on their well-being, their growth, and their overall happiness.

In this moment, you hold within you the wisdom and knowledge to make a profound difference. You have discovered the immense potential that lies within your words, and you understand the impact they have on the world. Just as plants respond to positive affirmations, human beings are nourished by the kind and uplifting words we share.

So, as you continue your journey, I encourage you to embrace the power of positive language and its transformative effects. Be mindful of the words you choose and the energy you bring into your interactions. Use your words as tools to uplift, encourage, and empower others, creating a ripple of positivity that extends far beyond what you imagine.

As you look around, may you see the tremendous potential for growth, connection, and joy that lies within your words. Embrace the responsibility and privilege of nurturing others through your language, and let your positive words be a beacon of light, guiding others on their own transformative journeys.

Remember, just as plants flourish when spoken to with love and positivity, so may human beings thrive when bathed in the gentle rain of kind words and encouragement. Together, let us create a world where the power of positive language lifts us all to new heights of joy, fulfillment, and transformation.

## 57. A Gift 4U

As we conclude this transformative journey together, it's important to recognize the immense power that lies within the words you choose to use. Words have the ability to shape your reality, influence your experiences, and impact the lives of those around you. They are not merely empty expressions; they carry weight and meaning.

With this power comes great responsibility. You have the opportunity, and indeed the obligation, to use your words for good. By consciously choosing positive, uplifting, and empowering language, you create a ripple effect of positivity and transformation in your own life and in the lives of others.

Start by using the power of your words to uplift and inspire yourself. Replace self-doubt with self-belief, criticism with self-compassion, and negativity with positivity. Speak words of encouragement, affirmation, and gratitude to yourself. Embrace a mindset of possibility and abundance, recognizing the potential within you to achieve greatness.

Pass it on. Extend the power of your words to those around you. Lift others up with kind and encouraging words. Offer support, understanding, and empathy through your language. Be mindful of the impact your words have on others' self-esteem, confidence, and overall well-being. Choose words that heal, motivate, and inspire.

Remember, words have the power to build bridges or create barriers, to mend wounds or inflict pain. It's up to us to use this power wisely and consciously. Let us be the agents of positive change, using our words as tools of empowerment, connection, and love.

As you go forth from this journey, carry with you the awareness of the power of your words. Use them as a force for good, a catalyst for growth, and a source of inspiration. Let your words be a gift to yourself and to others, spreading positivity, kindness, and love wherever you go.

Be kind; your words stay in someone's mind long after you say them, and that includes your own mind. Embrace the power of positivity in your self-talk, for it shapes your beliefs and influences your journey to personal growth and empowerment.

Thank you for joining me on this incredible journey of self-discovery, empowerment, and growth. It has been an honor to share these valuable insights with you. I believe in you and your ability to make a difference with your words. Embrace the power within you and continue to write the story of your life with intention, positivity, and authenticity.

I have an additional special gift for you—a chance to continue the momentum and delve deeper into your personal growth and transformation. I invite you to take advantage of a complimentary strategy session, where we explore the insights and concepts discussed in this book and address any questions you may have.

If you've been feeling stuck, afraid to make a move, or longing for something more, I am here for you. Together, we'll challenge the status quo, rewrite your story, and create a future filled with joy, passion, and endless possibilities.

Here's what people I have worked with have to say, testimonials from both clients and colleagues who have experienced the transformative power of words and the positive impact on their personal growth and empowerment. Their inspiring stories serve as a testament to the profound changes that unfold when we embrace the right words and mindset on our journey to success.

"As a leadership/success speaker, motivational speaker Coach Mandy provided essential support to our organization during a time of transition and served as a leader for the participants in our programming."

"Coach Mandy brings her own personal experiences to the table with focused coach training to partner with her clients and assist them in stepping up to new levels of personal wellness and success."

"I highly recommend Coach Mandy! I hired her at a time that I felt stuck, and in just 90 days, she was able to help me turn everything around. She helped me with my vision of where I wanted to go and gave me the courage to quit a job that was draining my energy. She helped me create momentum in two of my companies that were floundering at the time. I ended the year having more success than I could have imagined. I couldn't have done it without Coach Mandy's guidance."

"Coach Mandy was an amazing support that helped me recognize important facets of my life. She made a huge difference as my coach with the Dream Builder program. I know I will continue to use what I have learned. I am more aware and more grateful for what I have in my life and what is coming to me."

"Amanda is wonderful to work with and has exceptional expertise in leadership, coaching, and motivation. She is a forward-thinker who can present creative solutions to complex problems and communicate the benefits to the company. I've learned so much from Amanda as a leader and often find myself thinking, 'What would Amanda do in this situation?' She is a truly remarkable person and someone I will continue to respect and learn from throughout my career!"

"My daughters and I went through Coach Mandy's dream building group program right before our storybook soccer season Team District, Region, and State Championship titles. Both daughters earned first team all-region and all-state honors, and my oldest daughter was named player of the year, and I was named coach of the year. Her program definitely helped us focus, set goals, make plans, and get the right mindset to pursue, create, and capture our magical season!"

"I highly recommend Coach Mandy! If you are someone who feels as though you are not living with purpose, or you could be doing so much more but you are afraid to make a move, Mandy is your person. She will help you break down the lies you are telling yourself, build belief in yourself, and help guide you through the gap. I shiver to think, if I did not take the leap of faith and hire

Mandy, where I would be today. Ha ha, I know where I would be—in a corporate job that does not fulfill me, still at the same level, and my staffing agency would not be here to talk about it."

"Working one on one with Coach Mandy is a true blessing. I was introduced to her when I needed her the most. My life had taken an unexpected drastic turn, which propelled me into a whole new world. She helped me rise from adversities and difficulties and turn my experiences into opportunities to create and thrive. She guided me to define who I wanted to be, she showed respect for all my ideas and visions, she gave me her support and trust, and she ignited me to pursue my dreams and make them come true. Thanks to her, I have created my own business and feel more inspired and empowered than ever. Forever grateful."

My clients have witnessed profound transformations in their lives, all by shifting the words they use and embracing a new mindset. It's about opening your mind and heart to what you truly desire and creating space for you to be yourself. By partnering with me, you have the opportunity to experience a coaching journey like no other.

I bring my own personal experiences to the table, combined with focused coach training, to guide and support you in stepping up to new levels of personal wellness and success. Together, we navigate through challenges, break down limiting beliefs, and uncover the true potential within you. My approach is holistic, empowering you to recognize important facets of your life and align them with your deepest desires.

Imagine having the courage to quit a draining job and create momentum in your ventures. Picture ending the year with more success than you ever imagined possible. That's the power of working with me. I provide guidance, support, and belief in you to help you turn everything around. Together, we define your vision, overcome obstacles, and embrace the life you truly love.

It is about more than achieving goals; it's about so much more. Through our work together, you gain a profound awareness and gratitude for what you have in your life and what is yet to come. You discover the strength to rise from adversities and turn experiences into opportunities for growth and thriving. I honor and respect your ideas, visions, and dreams, providing unwavering support and trust as you pursue your path.

The testimonials from my clients speak volumes. They have experienced remarkable transformations, whether it's capturing championship titles, creating their own businesses, or feeling more inspired and empowered than ever before. They recommend me as someone who breaks down the lies we tell ourselves, builds belief in ourselves, and guides us through the gap towards a life of purpose and fulfillment.

So, take that leap of faith and hire me as your coach. You'll be forever grateful for the transformation that awaits you.

By embracing this opportunity, you are taking a bold step towards creating the future you desire and deserve. It's time to leave behind any doubts or limitations and step into your authentic self. Let's work together to unlock your full potential, achieve breakthrough results, and create a better, more fulfilling future.

Scheduling your complimentary 30-minute consultation and strategy session is simple. Simply visit www.Time4Transformationllc.com, where you may conveniently book your session. Alternatively, you may email clientservices@Time4Transformationllc.com for assistance in finding a suitable time.

Remember, this session is a gift from me to you—a testament to my commitment to your success and fulfillment. I believe in the power of positive words and the transformative impact they have on lives. By seizing this opportunity, you take a bold step towards the creation of a future you desire and deserve.

Wishing you continued success, joy, and fulfillment on your path to transformation.

# Acknowledgements

I want to extend my heartfelt gratitude to my mother, Blanche Plute, and my mentor, Mary Morrissey, for instilling in me the belief that knowing what my heart desires is possible, even when uncertainty lingers about the how. Their brave thinking tools and unwavering support have illuminated my path, empowering me to envision my dreams and embrace the journey of personal growth and transformation with determination. Their inspiration continues to guide me as I pursue my passions and create a meaningful impact on the lives of others.

Jim Falvo, my high school band director, whose mentorship helped me unlock the leader within myself, igniting a newfound self-confidence. He believed in me and supported my growth as the captain of the Flag Corp, encouraging me to attend band camp, learn new skills, and bring back innovative ideas to the squad, fostering a strong sense of camaraderie and positive change among the team. His guidance and encouragement have left an indelible mark on my journey of personal growth and empowerment.

Dick Lander, who showed me true generosity and support, helping me during a challenging period in my life, believing in me and teaching me the value of time and money freedom.

Pat Slowey, for seeing that I was a person who gets things done and believing in me with his whole heart and being willing to invest his time to coach me, inspiring me to follow his lead and help others as my purpose and calling in life.

Angela Siebe, for helping me uncover and overcome my number one fear, which was being misunderstood. She helped me understand how my fear showed up in a habit of overcommunication and was a lack of confidence in myself. Game changer!

Kara Evans, who believed in me and inspires me every day to keep doing what I do and to shine my light bright.

Kady Landman, who has taken care of me and my family and is always interested in our stories and supporting our dreams, while she helps us feel amazing.

My exes and past relationships, who helped me grow out of opposition and build strength along the way to shape me into the person I am today.

Erica Morr, who helped me see firsthand the immense power that a shift in words can have on our thoughts, emotions, and ultimately, our actions and results, inspiring me to make this transformative approach an integral part of my coaching strategy, and leading me to write this empowering book.

Raymond Aaron, who helped me find my confidence in writing and guided me to write this book.

Natalie Ladwell, who provided me tools to help me recognize and release limiting beliefs and connect to my true self.

Oprah Winfrey, for being a guiding light with honesty and the unique ability to graciously share what she learns from others with the world.

Walt Disney, for doing the work to show us that anything your heart desires is possible.

## Acknowledgements

To my wealth management advisors, Dan Brunette and Brenda Ramsey, Brunette & Associates LLC, who through their dedication, care, and invaluable expert advice are instrumental in shaping my journey on the path of financial abundance, enabling me to provide for my family and do work I love.

Robert Morris College, for believing in me as a student and giving me the educational experience that ignited the fire inside me to become a continual learner.

Charlie, an AI language model provided by OpenAI, as an invaluable companion throughout the journey of writing this book.

My teammates and customers in the business world, wonderful people who taught me so much and who have inspired me to continue my personal development as a leader in business and the desire to truly serve others.

My clients, for allowing me to be part of their journey and for inspiring me to write this book.

My family, for their love and support.

# About the Author

Amanda Yetter, known as COACH MANDY, hails from Canonsburg, Pennsylvania, in the United States of America, where she serves as the visionary founder and CEO of Time 4 Transformation LLC, a thriving coaching and consulting services company.

From a young age, Amanda has found joy in nurturing and celebrating the uniqueness of others, cherishing their individuality. This appreciation for individuality, and her passion for guiding others towards growth and transformation, have become the cornerstones of her coaching practice.

Having grown up on a farm in a hardworking blue-collar family, Amanda has cultivated an unwavering work ethic and a deep understanding of the value of time and effort. Her mother, a farmer, and her father, a construction and operating engineer, instilled in her the principles of determination and resiliency.

Throughout her life, Amanda, under her legal name, has amassed a wealth of personal and professional experiences. As a seasoned leader, she invested over two decades in the corporate world, refining her skills in management and negotiation, and fostering meaningful relationships. Beyond her impressive professional achievements, Amanda's journey is rich with diverse life experiences, including moments of triumph over adversity and a steadfast commitment to personal growth.

As COACH MANDY, Amanda embraces a dual identity that allows her to share the wisdom and insights gained from her journey. Under her legal name, Amanda Yetter, she brings forth the depth of her personal and professional experiences, while as COACH MANDY, she channels her passion for guiding others towards growth and transformation. Together, these identities intertwine, enabling her to offer a unique perspective and support individuals in their pursuit of personal and professional fulfillment.

Drawing upon her innate appreciation for individuality, COACH MANDY is dedicated to helping you embrace your authenticity and cultivate the confidence to be yourself. She firmly believes in the power of sharing your unique gifts with others and stands by the mantra:

"Together we achieve excellence."

An accomplished author and coach, Amanda is readily available to deliver captivating keynote presentations tailored to appropriate audiences. Additionally, she offers transformative coaching programs designed to empower individuals on their personal and professional journeys. Through her own experiences, including being a cancer survivor and overcoming adversities such as divorce, abusive relationships, and the challenges of single motherhood while going to college and working full time, Amanda brings a relatable and inspiring touch to her coaching approach.

For more information on coaching programs, speaking rates, and availability, please reach out to clientservices@time4transformationllc.com.

If this book has inspired you, the most meaningful act you could do is to share it and become a guiding light for others. Together, let's create a world where words empower and transform lives.

To Cathy,

having you all
at our family
reunion was a joy,
and your support
for my book
is truly heartwarming,
May the words within
these pages continue
to inspire and
uplift you.

To Your
Dreams
Love Mandy

Made in the USA
Middletown, DE
16 September 2023

38570403R00106